EAST AFRICA

LILA PERL

EAST AFRICA

KENYA
TANZANIA
UGANDA

illustrated with 58 photographs
William Morrow and Company
New York   1973

Library of Congress Catalog Card Number 73-4927
ISBN 0-688-20088-5
ISBN 0-688-30088-X (lib. bdg.)
1 2 3 4 5 77 76 75 74 73

All photographs are by Lila Perl with the exception of the following: United
Nations, pages 12, 75, 76, 81, 82, 84, 91, 101, 104, 105, 114, 123, 130, 139, 148, 151,
152; Kenya Ministry of Information, pages 14, 16, 32, 37, 44, 47, 48, 53, 55, 56, 61,
126, 127, 145, back jacket; Uganda Tourist Board, pages 24, 64, 98, 106, 108, 110.
Permission is gratefully acknowledged.

Front jacket photo: A woman of eastern Kenya's Giriama tribe
Back jacket photo: Mount Kilimanjaro

BY THE SAME AUTHOR
Ethiopia, Land of the Lion

ACKNOWLEDGMENTS

The author wishes to express her gratitude to the following for their generous assistance and valued cooperation:

Mr. J. L. Shako, Minister of Tourism and Wildlife, Kenya; Mr. Philip Mullei, Senior Tourist Officer, Nairobi; Mr. James O. Ochoki, Tourist Officer, Kenya Tourist Office, New York; Mr. J. J. Karuku, Tourist Information Officer, Nairobi; Mr. Joseph Chege, Assistant Tourist Officer, Mombasa; Mr. P. Olindo, Director of Kenya National Parks; Kenya Ministry of Natural Resources; Mr. E. Matu, Deputy Director of Information, Kenya Ministry of Information and Broadcasting; Mr. S. Mulokozi, Tanzania Mission to the United Nations, New York; Uganda Tourist Board; Uganda Hotels Limited; Uganda National Parks; United Touring Company, Kampala; Uganda Mission to the United Nations, New York; Mr. Walter Menke, Trans World Airlines; Mrs. Lis K. Brewer, Hilton International; Mr. Thomas Letham, General Manager, Nairobi Hilton Hotel.

CONTENTS

I
THE LANDSCAPE

From the Isle of Cloves to the Mountains of the Moon, from the scorching shores of Lake Rudolf to the chilly depths of Lake Malawi. . . . Between these romantically named places with their sharply contrasting landscapes lies the territory known as East Africa.

Today this territory consists of three independent and steadily changing African nations: Kenya, Tanzania, and Uganda. Together these countries occupy about 680,000 square miles, an area nearly one fifth the size of the United States.

The East African land mass stretches northward to the borders of Somalia, Ethiopia, and the Sudan. On the west it is bounded by Zaire (formerly Democratic Republic of the Congo), Rwanda, and Burundi, and on the south by Zambia, Malawi, and Mozambique. To the east lies the Indian Ocean,

In Uganda's mist-shrouded Ruwenzori Mountains

the earliest means of access to East Africa, and the gateway for most of the traders, slavers, missionaries, explorers, and empire builders that figured in East Africa's turbulent past and whose influence is still encountered in its bewildering present.

For most parts of East Africa, recorded time began as recently as the 1860's. And for its three independent countries, nationhood came as recently as the 1960's. During the preceding centuries, back to the beginning of historical record keeping in other parts of the world, East Africa was a source of myth and speculation to foreign civilizations.

In the second century A.D., Ptolemy, the Greco-Egyptian geographer and astronomer, drew a map of East Africa showing the Lunae Montes, or Mountains of the Moon. He believed that the melting snows of these soaring mountains, deep in the heart of Africa, fed the mighty Nile River, which flowed north through Egypt and emptied into the Mediterranean Sea.

Ptolemy is believed to have based this information on the travel reports of Diogenes, a first-century Greek merchant, who apparently ventured inland from the East African coast but in all probability got no farther west than Mount Kenya or Mount Kilimanjaro, neither of which feeds the Nile.

Nevertheless, Ptolemy's Mountains of the Moon, or the Ruwenzori as they now are called, do exist, forming part of the western boundary of Uganda and of the territory of East Africa. The Ruwenzori foothills are lushly forested, while the higher peaks of the sixty-mile-long range are mist-shrouded and permanently snowcapped. Mount Margherita in the Ruwenzori Range is the third highest mountain in Africa (16,763 feet), after Mount Kilimanjaro and Mount Kenya.

Ptolemy was correct, too, in his assumption that the Lunae Montes fed the Nile, for the tumbling streams of the Ruwenzori do flow indirectly into Lake Albert and so into the Albert Nile. However, the true source of Ptolemy's information, obtained 1800 years ago, about a mountain range at the core of an unknown and largely inaccessible continent remains a mystery to this day.

Not quite such a mystery is the coral island of Zanzibar, the Isle of Cloves, which lies in the Indian Ocean about twenty-two miles off the coast of East Africa. As early as the tenth century A.D., the offshore islands of Zanzibar, Pemba, and Lamu and the immediate coastal area were being visited by Arabs, Indians, Persians, and Far Eastern peoples who sailed to Africa on the favorable monsoon winds of the Indian Ocean. Zanzibar, a tropical island with coconut palms, a busy harbor, and feverish trading life, became the principal jumping-off point for excursions into the interior. When one of its sultan rulers established a flourishing clove industry there, Zanzibar earned the name, Isle of Cloves.

A variety of extraordinary natural features lies between the Isle of Cloves and the Mountains of the Moon.

At the equator in the Kenyan highlands,
showing temperate-zone landscape

The equator crosses East Africa, slicing through the southerly halves of what are now Kenya and Uganda, while all of Tanzania lies just south of the equator. East Africa's equatorial location gives most people the impression that it is a land of dense jungle and sultry climate, similar to many parts of West Africa. Ptolemy's positioning of the snowcapped Ruwenzori peaks caused general disbelief and even amusement over the centuries. How could there be snow on the equator?

This phenomenon was, of course, possible because of the high elevations of these mountains, which, like most others in East Africa, are of volcanic origin. Mount Kilimanjaro, which means *shining mountain* in the local tribal tongue, boasts the highest peak in Africa: Kibo, at 19,340 feet. Mount Kilimanjaro also has a lesser peak, Mawenzi, at 16,896 feet. The two Kilimanjaro peaks are connected by a long ridge.

Mount Kenya, at 17,058 feet, is Africa's second highest mountain. Although it sits almost astride the equator, it has formidable ice caves and glacial formations. It lies in what is

Opposite: A narrow street on Zanzibar, the Isle of Cloves

Looking skyward up a glacial crevasse in Mount Kenya

today Kenya, while Kilimanjaro lies just across the border in Tanzania. The story is often repeated in present-day Africa of how, at the onset of British and German colonialism, Queen Victoria had a hump drawn in the otherwise straight border line between British-controlled Kenya and German-controlled Tanganyika (now Tanzania) so that Kaiser Wilhelm II could have a tall snowcapped mountain of his own as a birthday present. Kaiser Wilhelm was Victoria's grandson.

Other prominent peaks in East Africa are Mount Meru in northern Tanzania (14,979 feet) and Mount Elgon in eastern Uganda on the border with Kenya (14,178 feet). These upward-thrusting masses tell us that much of East Africa is made up of elevated terrain—misty green hill country, high plateaus of tawny grassland, scattered woodland, and barren semidesert dotted with thorny scrub. At elevations of 3000 and 7000 feet, daytime temperatures range between a comfortable 70 and 85 degrees Fahrenheit, dropping to about 50 degrees at night. On the higher inhabited slopes of the mountains, nighttime temperatures dip as low as 30 degrees.

Almost the only place in East Africa where the expected hot equatorial climate is to be found is along the Indian Ocean. However, the 825-mile-long coastal belt, with its palms and flowering tropical plants, its mangrove swamps, intense humidity, and high rainfall, is only 10 to 40 miles deep along the eastern edges of Kenya and Tanzania. Although freshened by breezes from the vast Indian Ocean, temperatures along the coastal strip do range between 85 and 100 degrees.

There are dramatic differences between the steamy climate of Tanzania's capital of Dar es Salaam, situated on the coast 10 feet above sea level, and the cool temperate climate of Kenya's central-highland capital of Nairobi. The latter lies at an elevation of over 5000 feet.

The land mass occupied by Kenya, Tanzania, and Uganda is notable for its record-making geographical features. In addition to having the three tallest mountains on the continent, East Africa boasts the world's second largest lake: Lake Victoria. Only Lake Superior, in North America, is larger. Victoria covers an area of 26,828 square miles and is about equal in size to the republic of Ireland. Today the joined borders of Kenya, Tanzania, and Uganda lie somewhere in the waters of Lake

Victoria, and each country possesses a portion of the lake's shoreline.

The most important geographic influence on the East African landscape is the Great Rift Valley, a 4000-mile-long troughlike fissure in the earth's surface, which runs on a diagonal plane in a southwesterly direction. Starting in the Middle East, the Rift opening passes beneath the Red Sea and cuts through Ethiopia. It enters northern Kenya at Lake Rudolf, a large but shrinking lake, set in a treeless world of black lava rock and blistering hot winds.

The Rift then divides into two great arms. The Eastern Rift descends through Kenya on a north-south course. About 30 miles west of Nairobi, there are breathtaking views of the Rift Valley. The earth drops away abruptly from an elevation of 7000 feet to about 5200 feet. It is so chilly along the windy ridge overlooking the bottom land that the local people are

The top of the escarpment overlooking the Rift Valley in Kenya

often clad in sheepskins—at approximately one degree south
of the equator!

The Eastern Rift continues south through Tanzania, where
it creates less extreme formations. At Lake Manyara, in northern Tanzania, the escarpment to the west is fairly steep, but
east of the lake it slopes upward very gradually. Lake Manyara
itself lies in the trough of the Rift Valley.

The Western Rift traces a semicircular course around the
western border of East Africa in what is now Uganda. This
arm can be identified by a string of Rift Valley lakes: Albert,
George, and Edward. Lakes Albert and Edward are shared by
Uganda and Zaire, while Lake George lies wholly within
Uganda.

The Western Rift continues its curving and deepening course,
reaching Lake Tanganyika on Tanzania's western border. This
lake has the distinction of being the longest in the world (420
miles), the second deepest in the world (over 4700 feet; only
Lake Baikal in Siberia is deeper), and the second largest lake in
Africa (after lake Victoria). Lake Tanganyika's coastline is
steep-sided and has few natural harbors.

At Lake Malawi, in southern Tanzania, the eastern and
western arms of the Rift come together. This lake is shared by
Tanzania and the neighboring states of Malawi (formerly Ny-
asaland) and Mozambique, and it is the third largest lake in
Africa. It was formerly called Lake Nyasa, which was simply
the local tribal word for *lake*. In the days when Europeans
spoke of it as Lake Nyasa, they were actually calling it Lake
Lake.

Lake Victoria is not part of the Rift system but lies in the
basin of a high plateau between the eastern and western arms.
Victoria is shallow—only about 270 feet deep—and is liberally
dotted with islands, particularly near its shores. At Ripon Falls,

the Nile flows out and begins its 4000-mile journey to the Mediterranean Sea. Today this immense gush of water has been harnessed through the construction of Owen Falls Dam to serve as a source of electrical power throughout much of East Africa. The dam, located on the northern shore of Lake Victoria at the town of Jinja, in Uganda, was completed in 1954.

After leaving the lake, the Victoria Nile, as the river now is called, flows into the shallow, sprawling, swamplike Lake Kyoga in central Uganda. From Kyoga it makes its way in a general northwesterly direction and over the broad, boiling rapids of Karuma Falls. Forty miles farther west, at Murchison Falls, the Nile casts itself into a 20-foot-wide rocky cleft. Here the already great river tumbles 140 feet into the pool below. The cataract creates a misty spray that remains suspended in the atmosphere like smoke, and its impact coats the water for some distance downstream with broad pads of multiple yellow bubbles.

The Nile then enters Lake Albert where it gathers added vigor, emerges as the Albert Nile, and flows north across the Uganda border into the Sudan. Here it becomes known as the White Nile. At Khartoum in the Sudan, the White Nile is joined by the Blue Nile, which flows into it from Ethiopia. And so, the great stream, now known simply as the Nile, flows on toward Egypt and the Mediterranean Sea.

The East African land mass appears to have comparatively few natural resources such as minerals, petroleum, and other raw materials of modern industrial value, although Uganda has copper mines near its western border and Tanzania has an important diamond mine. Even navigable rivers, which might serve for transport and trade, are almost nonexistent in East Africa.

In addition, agricultural development has been limited. One drawback has been the lack of sufficient rainfall over large stretches of inland terrain. East Africa has no true winter or summer seasons, only rainy and dry seasons. In inland areas with moderate rainfall there are generally two rainy seasons. The long rains fall between April and June, the short rains in November and December.

However, the rains do not always arrive on schedule, and often when they do they are too sparse. The resulting drought brings severe hardship to farmers and herders and to the vast wildlife population. In the very low-rainfall areas (under twenty inches annually), such as northern Kenya, northern Uganda, and much of central Tanzania, there is usually only one long season of scattered rainfall, which provides just enough water for some stock raising but makes farming a great risk or totally impossible.

Uganda is more fortunate than its two East African neighbors, for water evaporating from Lake Victoria falls as rain on the western side of the lake. As a result, Uganda has a much larger proportion of green and cultivated countryside than either Kenya or Tanzania. East Africa's rains, even at the coast, are not of the steady all-day variety but fall as showers, broken daily by long periods of sunshine.

The presence of the tsetse fly has been another serious drawback to extensive farming and herding in East Africa. The tsetse fly inhabits the dry brush and thickets of the scattered woodlands that extend over much of the elevated inland country. It looks like an ordinary large housefly except that its wings are crossed at the back. The tsetse lives on blood, has a painful bite, and is a transmitter of germs known as trypanosomes, which cause serious illnesses: nagana in domestic stock and sleeping sickness in human beings. Wild animals, on the other hand, have good resistance to the bites of trypanosome-carrying insects.

In Tanzania, extensive upland plateau regions, estimated to be as much as 60 percent of the country, are "under the fly" and therefore uninhabitable by man or livestock animals. Dry wooded regions of Kenya and Uganda are also infested but by much smaller percentages. Systematic clearing of the dense brush in which the shade-loving tsetse fly breeds is an important step toward increasing land productivity.

A ten-foot-tall termite hill near Lake Manyara in Tanzania

Other serious insect pests of East Africa are locusts, whose periodic invasions can destroy crops over a vast area. Safari, or traveler, ants are another menace. These ferocious reddish-brown insects travel in long chains and will devour any and all small animals encountered in their line of march. Chickens kept in coops are easy victims. Caged rabbits and other creatures unable to escape meet a similar fate. Elephants that accidentally sweep safari ants off the ground and into their trunks become maddened and highly dangerous.

A regular feature of the East African landscape is the termite hills, as common as the thorny flat-topped umbrella acacia trees and the candelabralike euphorbia trees that dot the upland plateaus. The fortresslike termite mounds are often ten feet or more in height and are made of earth mixed with partially digested cellulose, a product of the termites' diet of wood.

The sunbaked mounds are stone-hard on the outside. Inside they are galleried and even have ducts leading into the earth. These ducts help maintain proper temperature and humidity levels within the mound. The ten thousand or more termite inhabitants inside the dark mound even grow their own fungus for food. Mounds that appear as small pimples of earth on the surface of the grassy plains can grow with astonishing speed, attaining the height of a man in about six months. It is believed that termites are the most numerous of all insects in Africa.

Probably East Africa's greatest natural wealth lies in its immense wildlife population. The grassy high plains support huge herds of zebra and many varieties of antelope—wildebeest, topi, hartebeest, gazelle, impala, eland, oribi, kudu, waterbuck, kob, and, the tiniest of all, the eight- to ten-pound dik-dik.

Zebra and antelope, in turn, are food for the meat-eating animals—the lions, leopards, cheetahs, and other cats—as well

Eland in Tanzania's Ngorongoro Crater

as for the scavengers—the jackals, hyenas, wild dogs, vultures, and marabou storks that clear away the leavings of the hunting animals and occasionally make their own kills of smaller or helpless animals.

The dignified giraffe graces open country that is dotted with acacia trees, upon which it feeds, while the quick-stepping warthog grovels in mud and hides its warty face and small rotund body in burrows in the ground. The wooded regions of the high plateaus are the home of elephant and buffalo, while crocodiles and hippopotamuses live in and near the lakes, rivers, and swampy areas.

The rhinoceros, both the black and the white variety, is found in East Africa. The white rhino is even larger than the black and is a rarer species, being found only in Uganda where it is indigenous west of the Albert Nile. Actually both black and white rhinos are gray in color. The term *white* is believed to come from the Afrikaans language of South Africa and was originally intended to mean *wide,* as this type of rhino has a broad mouth and a square jaw, more like that of a hippo.

East Africa's birds are as spectacular as its four-legged beasts and add up to many hundreds of species. Ostriches, flightless and the largest birds in the world, are a common sight on the plains. To make up for their inability to fly, they are swift runners and can attain speeds up to forty-five miles per hour. Ostriches are preyed upon by lions but sometimes elude them by swerving abruptly while keeping up a fast running pace.

The long-legged secretary bird, with its white breast feathers and black tail section, wears a clutch of feathers behind its head. It is so named because these feathers resemble the quill pens that office clerks at one time carried behind their ears. Crested cranes, with their black-and-white bodies accented with red and their tufted golden crowns, are extraordinarily handsome. Waterbirds are numerous. Flamingos inhabit ponds and shallow lakes that are rich in mineral salts. Their formations appear as broad, sweeping ribbons of delicate pink on the still surface of the water. The eggs and fledglings of flamingos are the prey of marabou storks, while ostrich eggs are often eaten by vultures, which crack them open by dropping rocks from their beaks onto the eggs.

Starlings in many varieties are among the most colorful of all East Africa's smaller birds, flashing through the trees in streaks of iridescent blue and copper. Less easily spotted is the small, gray-brown honey guide. This bird has a talent for locating the nests of wild bees in trees but is unable to probe its way into the hive. It transmits its information to one of two creatures—the honey badger and man.

Africans tell many stories about their encounters with the honey guide. Once a man has responded to the bird's insistent chattering, followed its flight to the bees' nest, smoked out the bees and removed the honey, he must leave something of the hive behind for the honey guide, which feeds on beeswax and

larvae. According to legend, if the honey hunter is so ungrateful
as to leave nothing for the honey guide, the bird will at some
future time again entice him into the forest, and this time he
will lead him to harm and eventual disaster.

Some of East Africa's birds and mammals live in close physical relationship. Oxpeckers spend most of their time perched
on the bodies of giraffes, rhinos, and buffaloes, eating ticks,
flies, and even bits of the animal's external body tissue. Elephants, with their long-reaching trunks, do not permit such
steady company. The egrets and other birds seen on or near
these great beasts are there to pounce on the insects and other
small creatures disturbed by the movement of the large animal
through the grass.

Elephants accompanied by an egret in
Uganda's Murchison Falls National Park

Monkeys and baboons are common in East Africa, particularly the small, gray vervet monkey with its black, heart-shaped face rimmed in white. Colobus monkeys, however, are not so often seen, as their long silky black-and-white fur has long been a favorite for tribal headdresses. Chimpanzees inhabit some of the forested areas, and the shy mountain gorilla keeps to the highlands of southwestern Uganda. As many specimens of this primate have been taken for zoos and for testing and observation purposes, the species has become rare in East Africa today.

For the most part, the East African landscape has been a primeval paradise for its wildlife population. This landscape has also offered a comfortable although limiting environment for East African man. Despite large stretches of arid countryside and numerous insect enemies, the indigenous peoples evolved a means of existence that worked well for them. The climate was favorable, food could be gathered, hunted, or grown in sufficient quantity, and suitable materials for clothing and shelter lay close at hand. Human population growth was controlled by natural means, and life went on through a series of minor adaptations, but without startling or dramatic change, for centuries.

II
THE PEOPLE

Man is believed to have lived in East Africa as far back as the dim reaches of prehistory. But only in the second half of the twentieth century did evidences of early human existence in this landscape come to light, proving not only the ancient presence of man but also indicating that East Africa very possibly may be the two-million-year-old birthplace of modern man. In northern Tanzania, at the eastern edge of the vast Serengeti wildlife plain, lies Olduvai Gorge, a fossil site that has revealed itself rich in information concerning man's origin.

The first European to report on the gorge was a German scientist, Professor Kattwinkel. In 1911, Kattwinkel was in Tanganyika, then known as German East Africa, collecting butterfly specimens. On one of his expeditions into the bush he came upon a deep ravine. Carefully examining its gravelly slopes, the professor found a number of animal fossil remains, including bones of an extinct three-toed horse, which he later took back with him to Germany for the Berlin Museum collection.

In the years that followed, other scientists visited Olduvai Gorge. Their diggings unearthed the bones of other extinct animals: a pig as large as a hippo, with tusks three feet long; a peculiar elephant with tusks that pointed downward; a giant sheep with horns spanning six feet. Geological studies revealed that the bottom of the gorge once had been a lake with a surrounding lowland rich in vegetation and animal life, very different from the parched, stony landscape that Olduvai Gorge occupies today. Nearly two million years ago, volcanic eruptions deposited lava and ash over the lake area. Later, clays, sands, and silt were deposited and the earth's surface began to build up. Then, about 30,000 years ago, strong earth tremors opened a 200-foot-deep chasm on the site of the old lakeshore. The abrupt walls of the chasm exposed layers of rock-hard

The fossilized skull of a prehistoric
giant sheep found in Olduvai Gorge

material, like a series of shelves, each layer telling its story of a period of prehistory.

For study purposes, geologists have divided the gorge walls into five horizontal units, known as beds. Bed I represents the bottommost unit, composed of layers of volcanic ash and clay. It rests on the lava deposit that forms the floor of the gorge and is believed to date back 1,750,000 years.

In 1959, British Kenya-born anthropologist, Doctor Louis Leakey, and his wife, Mary, also an anthropologist, were working in Bed I when Mrs. Leakey came upon a bit of bone from the skull of a hominid, a form of preman. The crushed skull was in hundreds of tiny pieces but was eventually assembled. Its owner was given the name *Zinjanthropus*. This creature had a large skull but a small brain. Its teeth revealed that it was probably a vegetarian, as are most of the apes. Although not a direct ancestor, *Zinjanthropus,* a composite ape-man, is believed to have been a cousin to the direct link to man.

In 1960, continuing their work in Bed I, the Leakeys came upon the fossilized bones of a group of contemporaries of *Zinjanthropus.* The new specimens revealed a larger braincase, a foot with the big toe close to the others instead of separated as among the apes, and a well-articulated hand. This fossil form was termed *Homo habilis,* "the man with ability," for it was believed to indicate a primitive man who was a relatively accomplished toolmaker and tool user. While *Zinjanthropus,* having been a less adaptable form, apparently died out long, long ago, *Homo habilis* is considered to be a one-and-three-quarter-million-year-old direct ancestor of modern man.

The original of the *Zinjanthropus* skull is now in the National Museum in Dar es Salaam. A copy of the skull, along with some of the original prehistoric animal bones, is on display in the small museum on the site of Olduvai Gorge. The Leakeys

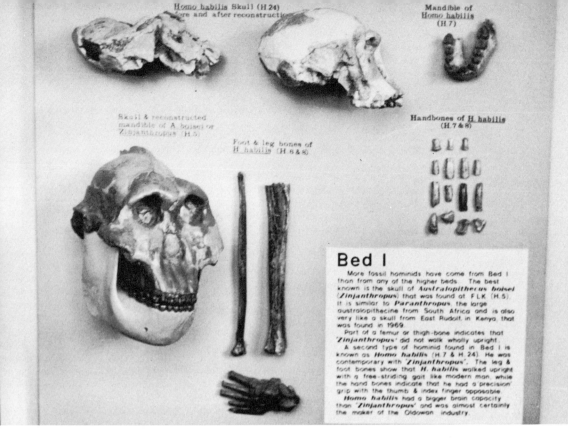

Homo habilis Skull (H 24) ...re and after reconstruct...

Mandible of Homo habilis (H 7)

Skull & reconstructed mandible of A. boisei or Zinjanthropus (H.5)

Handbones of H. habilis (H.7 & 8)

Foot & leg bones of H. habilis (H.8 & 8)

Bed I

More fossil hominids have come from Bed I than from any of the higher beds. The best known is the skull of *Australopithecus boisei* (*Zinjanthropus*) that was found at F.L.K. (H.5). It is similar to *Paranthropus*, the large australopithecine from South Africa and is also very like a skull from East Rudolf, in Kenya, that was found in 1969.

Part of a femur or thigh-bone indicates that '*Zinjanthropus*' did not walk wholly upright.

A second type of hominid found in Bed I is known as *Homo habilis* (H.7 & H.24). He was contemporary with '*Zinjanthropus*'. The leg & foot bones show that *H. habilis* walked upright with a free-striding gait like modern man, while the hand bones indicate that he had a 'precision' grip with the thumb & index finger opposable.

Homo habilis had a bigger brain capacity than '*Zinjanthropus*' and was almost certainly the maker of the Oldowan industry.

The reconstructed skulls of *Zinjanthropus* (lower left) and *Homo habilis* (above right), showing differences in sizes of brain cases

have since discovered fossils of other, much older forms of preman in East Africa, in diggings at Fort Ternan in Kenya, and on Rusinga Island in Lake Victoria. Doctor Leakey died in 1972, but other members of his family are continuing their work in the rich fossil beds of Olduvai Gorge. To date, the discovery of *Homo habilis* remains the most meaningful for modern man, who, it appears, now can trace his birthplace to East Africa.

Large gaps exist in our knowledge of man's continuing history in East Africa, particularly between the era of *Homo habilis* and the time of the birth of Christ. It is believed that in about 4000 B.C. primitive tribal peoples were living in what is now Kenya, Tanzania, and Uganda. They neither practiced agriculture nor did they herd livestock. They existed solely by hunting game and trapping small animals and by gathering roots, berries, and other edible plant life, as well as insects.

About 2000 years ago, coinciding with the beginning of the Christian era, a more advanced people known as the Bantu began moving eastward and southward from the Congo region of central Africa. These migrations continued over hundreds of years. Some of the earlier inhabitants of East Africa were either absorbed or engulfed by the Bantu people, but most are believed to have fled south into heavily forested or desert regions. Today's Bushmen of the Kalahari Desert in southern Africa are probably descendants of these hunting and gathering folk.

The Bantu, with their knowledge of agriculture and their ability to work metals, gradually repopulated most of East Africa. In fact, Bantu peoples are distributed today over about three fourths of Africa south of the Sahara. In East Africa, they are by far the largest ethnic and language family.

Hamitic and Nilotic peoples followed the period of Bantu migrations into East Africa. The Hamites are believed to have evolved in Asia in the Tigris-Euphrates valley, which is located in what is now Iraq. Some spread to the fertile Nile delta region of North Africa and drifted southward along the Nile through Egypt and the Sudan to East Africa; others crossed directly to Africa from the Arabian peninsula, entering East Africa by way of Ethiopia.

Many of the Hamites who came south from Egypt intermarried with the dark-skinned Nilotic peoples of the Nile valley and became known as Nilo-Hamites. Unlike the black-skinned Bantu and Nilotic peoples, the original Hamites had light skins

and small, fine-boned features. Hamites are classified racially
as Caucasians.

These four groups—Bantu, Hamitic, Nilotic, and Nilo-
Hamitic—make up the major ethnic families to which most
East African tribal peoples belong. The languages of the many
tribes within a given family are related, just as Spanish, French,
and Italian are related to one another and rooted in Latin. But
between tribes of different ethnic families, there is usually a
very marked language barrier.

There are today over 200 tribes in East Africa: roughly 60
in Kenya, 100 in Tanzania, and 40 in Uganda. This number
includes some ethnic and language groups outside the Bantu-
Nilotic-Hamitic circle, such as the Sudanic peoples of northern
Uganda, the El Molo of northern Kenya, and the Khoisan of
Tanzania.

The El Molo, who live on the southern shore of Lake Rudolf,
are believed to be descendants of East Africa's primitive, pre-
Bantu people. Living in a sparse, blazing countryside, they subsist almost completely on the distasteful, alkaline lake water
and on lake fish, which they harpoon from crude rafts of lashed-
together palm trunks.

Tribal peoples of the Khoisan family are also, very probably,
remnants of East Africa's early hunters and gatherers. The
Dorobo, a Khoisan tribe of north central Tanzania, subsist on
honey, plant roots, and berries, and whatever game they are
able to snare or shoot with their poisoned arrows. The dwin-
dling numbers of both the El Molo and the Dorobo indicate
that they may be dying out.

The language of the Khoisan family is related to that of the
Bushmen and Hottentots of southern Africa. Khoisan tongues
are often referred to as "click languages" because their speech
involves a series of clicking sounds made in various parts of

Left: An El Molo mother and child living
on the southern shore of Lake Rudolf
Right: El Molo fishermen on Lake Rudolf

the mouth. These sounds function as parts of the words themselves. The click language, once heard, is unforgettable; it is also extremely difficult to imitate.

As recently as the mid-twentieth century, peoples from neighboring countries have spilled over into East Africa, due to unrest and tribal upheavals in their own newly independent countries. Among these are Pygmies from Zaire, now living in Uganda, and Watutsi from Rwanda, now in both Tanzania and Uganda.

The occupations, dwellings, and daily routines, puberty rituals and marriage customs, arts and religious beliefs of the 200 or more tribes of East Africa are similar in many respects, especially among groups stemming from the same ethnic families. When life styles are quite different, it is usually because of the natural environment in which the group lives, the traditional occupation practiced by the tribe, and the degree of exposure to Western civilization, as well as ethnic-family origin.

Most Bantu tribes are agricultural and include such progressive groups as Kenya's largest tribe, the Kikuyu. The Kikuyu, who today number two million in a population of eleven million, are cultivators of maize, coffee, wheat, and garden vegetables in the cool, green highlands north of Nairobi and around the slopes of Mount Kenya. Another major Bantu tribe, the Kamba, are traditionally stock raisers in the semiarid uplands that lie between Nairobi and the coast. In the past, before the Masai migrated southward, the Kamba cattle herders were often raided by their primitive pastoral neighbors, who belong to the Nilo-Hamitic family. Today the Kamba raise beef cattle for market on their grazing lands, whose grass is nourishing despite its dull yellow color, while the Kikuyu maintain dairy herds in the moister hill country. The Giriama, a principal Bantu tribe of Kenya's palm-fringed coastal belt, also keep dairy cattle, which they graze beneath the coconut palms. In addition, they raise maize, bananas, mangoes, and cashews, and they grow sisal, which is used for making ropes, sacking, and other goods requiring strong fibrous material.

Among Tanzania's many Bantu tribes, the prosperous Chagga were some of the first East Africans to come in contact with Europeans, and these progressive agriculturalists adapted quickly to European farming ideas. In the early 1900's, with the help of German Catholic missionaries, they began to grow coffee bushes beneath their banana trees. While bananas, of the green cooking variety, long had been a staple food among the Chagga, coffee soon became a profitable cash crop. The Chagga today have their own coffee-marketing cooperative and, like the Kikuyu in Kenya, have modernized their way of life considerably. They now number several hundred thousand. The Sukuma, another Bantu people, are Tanzania's largest tribe, numbering one and one-quarter million. They live southeast of Lake Victoria on lands that they have cleared of the tsetse fly and where they now grow grains, sweet potatoes, cassava, and peanuts for their own use, as well as cotton and rice to take to market.

The Bantu farming peoples of Uganda are among the most advanced in East Africa. When Arab traders, the first foreigners to reach the northwestern shore of Lake Victoria, arrived sometime around 1850, they discovered to their surprise that the local people were living in large, prosperous kingdoms totally isolated from the outside world. The most important kingdom was Buganda. It was centered in the vicinity of what is today

A Kikuyu farmers' roadside market in the Kenyan highlands

Kampala, the capital of Uganda, but its territory fanned out well to the west of the lakeshore. The other major Ugandan kingdoms of the day were Bunyoro to the northwest of Buganda, Toro to the west, Ankole to the southwest, and Busoga to the east on the northern shore of Lake Victoria. These five kingdoms contained the main Bantu peoples of what is today Uganda.

Buganda was ruled by a king, or *kabaka,* assisted by a council of chiefs. British explorer John Hanning Speke, who visited Buganda in 1862 on his second expedition into East Africa, was probably the first European to appear at the court of the *kabaka,* who dwelt in a large round palace with a peaked, grass-thatch roof that rose directly from the ground and soared to a height of forty feet or more. The palace interior was about fifty feet in diameter and was lined with support posts covered in a supple reddish-brown cloth, which was made from the bark of the wild fig tree by a special process of beating and stretching. Bark cloth was also used for draperies and bed coverings.

In addition to working bark cloth, the Baganda (the prefix *ba* refers to the people; the prefix *bu* to the kingdom) wove watertight baskets, created fine musical instruments, and built massive war canoes for use on Lake Victoria. The mainstay of their diet was the green banana, which was cooked to make *matoke,* a starchy, white porridgelike substance that looks and tastes very much like thick mashed potato without seasoning and which was eaten with meat or fish stews. Beer, also made from the bananas that grew so abundantly in the region, was drunk in large quantities both at court and in the villages of the local chiefs.

Speke spent several months at the court of the *kabaka* of Buganda, Mutesa I. He reported that, despite the advanced political organization of the kingdom and the skills of the peo-

A replica of the palace of the king of Buganda

ple, the Baganda had no system of writing or record keeping, no plows or wheeled devices. They followed a religion based on ancestor worship and showed little regard for human life. Speke was appalled by an incident in which Mutesa casually had a man shot simply to try out a gun that the explorer had presented to him.

Today the old kingdoms of Uganda no longer exist as political entities. But the Bantu peoples whose forebears were subjects of Mutesa and the other kings, and who now make up two thirds of Uganda's African population, still occupy the lush, green southern half of the country with its moist, balmy climate. They live on small farms where they grow bananas, of both the sweet and plantain (cooking) variety, as well as maize, cassavas, sweet potatoes, and many other fruits and vegetables.

Among the Nilotic, Hamitic, and Nilo-Hamitic peoples of

A Boran woman and her camels in Kenya's arid northern region

Kenya, Tanzania, and Uganda, there are some tribes that, like the Bantu, practice agriculture primarily. Most, however, are chiefly herders of cattle and other livestock. The Acholi and the Lango tribes of semiarid north central Uganda are a Nilotic people who herd cattle but also cultivate basic food crops such as millet, sorghum, maize, and cassava. Their Nilotic neighbors to the east, the Karamojong, have a primitive economy that is focused on their cattle, which provide them with the blood and milk that they drink. The Luo of Kenya are a more advanced Nilotic people. After migrating into East Africa by way of the Nile valley, they settled on the eastern shore of Lake Victoria where they became fishermen and farmers. The Luo are today the second largest tribe in Kenya, after the Kikuyu, numbering about one and a third million.

East Africa's Hamitic peoples are found mainly in northern Kenya near the Ethiopian border, where tribes like the Boran

and the Rendille, along with the neighboring Somali, roam the
arid scrublands to the east of Lake Rudolf in search of water
and pasturage for their camels, goats, and fat-tailed sheep.

The Nilo-Hamitic tribes include such groups as the Suk, the
Turkana, and the Masai. Handsome, intriguing people—tall,
lean, and fine-boned, with brown skins and straight, slender
features—most are seminomadic tribesmen who revere their
cattle and reckon their personal wealth and prestige by the size
of their herds. They consider growing grains or other plant
food beneath their dignity. However, they trade or sell some of
their animal products for farm products and beer, spears and
other metal objects, and for the cloth, beads, and jewelry with
which they adorn themselves. The Suk and the Turkana live
on the dry grazing plains of western Kenya near the Ugandan
border, just north of Mount Elgon, while the Masai occupy
southern Kenya and northern Tanzania.

Although houses with corrugated tin roofs and cement walls
now make their appearance in the East African countryside,
most tribal dwellings are still constructed from the traditional
materials found in the immediate natural surroundings. Among
the Giriama and other coastal peoples, large family houses are
built with roofs of palm-leaf thatch and red-clay walls braced
with uprights of mangrove poles from the nearby coastal
swamps. In the East African upcountry, however, whether in
Kenya, Tanzania, or Uganda, tribal dwellings usually consist
of several small huts clustered together to form a homestead.
The huts may be of the round beehive type, or they may be
square or rectangular. The walls are usually of clayey mud
plastered onto a framework of saplings or poles fashioned from
tree limbs or large branches. The roofs are of grass thatch,
reeds, or leaves. In Uganda, papyrus and elephant grass, which

grow abundantly near lakes and streams, are used for roofing.

Most Bantu farm families live directly on their *shamba* (farm), rather than in villages, and are largely self-supporting. On a tribal homestead, the "family" extends well beyond the Western concept of husband, wife, and children. An East African "family" is more likely to consist of a father with his unmarried children, his married sons, and their children if any. Also resident on the homestead may be the father's brothers, each with his unmarried children and married sons. The wives, although they too live and work in the household, are considered to be members of their own families of origin.

The roles of the various family members are clearly defined. The men do the heavy farmwork, although the women help with the weeding and harvesting as well as doing the cooking and other household chores and caring for the children. Children start at an early age to fetch water and gather firewood. Soon the boys are out herding the family livestock while the girls begin caring for their younger sisters and brothers.

Daily life among the Bantu farming peoples of present-day East Africa follows age-old patterns. The day's routine goes according to the sun, which is almost unvarying in its hours of rising and setting. Because East Africa is located at the equator, night and day each have twelve hours, with sunrise at about 6:30 a.m. and sunset at about 6:30 p.m. Farming peoples get up with the first light of dawn and eat a meal of porridge or cold leftovers from the night before. Work in the fields lasts until lunchtime, which is at 1:00 or 2:00. Afterward, the men may rest or return to their chores, depending on the demands of the season. The evening meal is eaten just after sunset at about 7:00. Once the sun drops behind the horizon in equatorial Africa darkness falls quickly, and the family retires soon after supper.

Ugali is the basic dish among Bantu peoples in most parts of East Africa. *Ugali* (or *posho,* as it is called in Uganda) is a stiff porridge made with water and maize flour. It also can be prepared with millet or cassava flour. In regions where the green banana is grown, *matoke* takes the place of *ugali.* These stiff mixtures are rolled into little balls with the fingers and dipped into a sauce or stew gravy. Bits of meat, fish, or vegetables served in the stew are pressed against the sides of the porridge ball and the whole thing is popped into the mouth at once. Sweet potatoes and cassavas are eaten boiled or roasted; peanuts are finely ground to give substance to stews and sauces.

Pombe (beer) can be made from maize, millet, sorghum, or sugarcane, as well as from bananas. The process takes about one week, and then the beer is ready to drink. Bantu peoples in Kenya and Tanzania distill *pombe* to make *chang'aa* and *moshi,* regional names for strong alcoholic beverages. In Uganda, banana beer, which is known as *mwenge,* is distilled to make a potent, colorless liquor called *waragi.* Although it is illegal nowadays to produce these highly intoxicating drinks without a license, many tribal peoples continue to prepare them at home in secret.

While homegrown farm products provide most of the family's food, items such as yard goods, blankets, beads, cooking pots, knives, tea, rice, and tobacco are all purchased at the *duka* or local general store. Traditionally these shops have been operated by families of Asians, who usually live in quarters at the back of the shop. The first Asian shopkeepers set up business in the coastal trading centers, gradually drifting inland to the remote upcountry. Most *dukas* have a veranda in front, which is usually occupied by an African tailor seated at a treadle-operated sewing machine. Here customers can have their newly purchased yard goods made up into blouses, skirts, dresses, trousers, shirts, or whatever they wish.

As the Bantu have adapted to modern life, many have discarded the old tribal styles of dress and ornamentation. The Kikuyu, for example, now wear contemporary Western clothing instead of blankets or other wraparound garments. The cowherds, who sleep out at night in the lush but chilly highland pastures attending the grazing cattle, dress in long, brown overcoats or raincoats with layers of sweaters underneath. Kikuyu women still trudge the mountain roads bent nearly double beneath loads of firewood or dried vegetation. Their burdens are secured to their bodies in traditional fashion, by means of leather bands tightly looped across their foreheads and cutting deeply just above the eyebrows, but they are clad in Western-style dresses and factory-made sweaters.

The Giriama women of the hot coastal belt prefer the *kitenge,* a large colorful rectangle of cloth that is wrapped like a sarong around the body, either just above the breasts or at the waist, while tall market baskets or gourds of home-made beer ride gracefully balanced atop their heads.

Many Bantu peoples like to combine elements of traditional dress with items of Western costume. Sukuma men, for example, often wear a loincloth over a pair of European shorts or trousers. Bantu women of Tanzania may wear a *kitenge* over a Western-style dress, either as a wraparound or loosely draped over one shoulder. The *kanga,* a simple rectangle of cloth similar to the *kitenge* but less decorative, is used everywhere as a sling for carrying babies on the back or at the hip.

Head coverings are almost always worn by East African Bantu women, especially when working in the fields under the hot sun or walking long distances along the dusty roads. The close-fitting bandanna is tied snugly across the head and knotted, while the more elaborate turban is draped and puffed. Shaved heads were once the fashion for women in some tribes, such as the Kikuyu. Otherwise Bantu women wear their hair cropped close to the head or they plait it neatly into numerous tiny braids that lie flat in straight rows.

Bantu men of East Africa dress almost exclusively in Western clothing. Some, especially in the remote countryside, still wear the *kanzu,* a long white garment similar to a nightshirt, introduced by the Arabs. In the coastal cities, the *kanzu* is worn mainly by Moslems. The white, brimless cap for men, also introduced by the Arab Moslems, is quite common now, particularly in Tanzania, as a sort of national dress and does not mean the wearer is a Moslem. Shoes, if they are worn at all by either

A Ugandan woman in *busuti* and turban

men or women, are almost always sandals with flat soles and leather thongs drawn between the toes.

Uganda's Bantu women today dress in the *busuti*. Although not of tribal origin, it has been called the national costume of Uganda. Actually, this graceful garment of brightly patterned or gauzy, pastel cloth shows the styling influence of British Victorian clothing and was no doubt introduced by missionaries of the late nineteenth century. The dress consists of a bodice with a square neckline and short sleeves that are gathered and peaked at the shoulder and a long, flowing skirt with a diagonally draped swathe of cloth running from the waist to the hip. The *busuti* requires seven yards of material and is usually made up to order by marketplace tailors. Worn with a matching or contrasting Congo turban, the *busuti* offers an exceptionally attractive sight along Uganda's country roads as well as in its towns and capital city.

In the past, all Bantu peoples followed the widespread East African custom of inflicting tribal identification marks upon their youth. Often these body alterations were made at the onset of adolescence as part of the tribal initiation rites. It was very common to make cuts on the face, chest, back, and other parts of the body, which were then treated so as to produce raised scar tissue. Kikuyu women and others had tattoos applied to their faces, such as rows of blue dots on the upper parts of the cheeks just beneath the eyes. The teeth might be filed to points; the lips or nose might be pierced to receive ornaments of ivory or bone. The Kikuyu followed the custom of stretching their earlobes so that large holes were torn in the centers and the circlet of outer skin dangled nearly to the shoulder. The lobe was then hung with heavy metal jewelry or with numerous beaded hoops. Ornaments also were attached to the upper part of the ear.

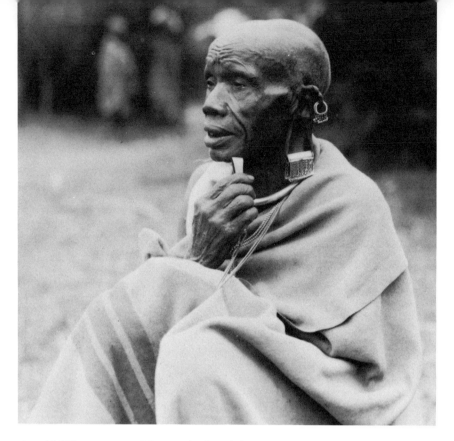

An old Kikuyu man with stretched earlobes

The puberty rites for both boys and girls were a major event in tribal life and still are practiced today by most Bantu tribes, although often in modified form. The Kikuyu and the Chagga at one time practiced female circumcision as well as male circumcision but now largely have discontinued the former, although some of the more traditional Bantu groups have not. Most initiation ceremonies involve intensive instruction on tribal matters and a test of endurance or strength, which is followed by a celebration that marks the passage into adulthood. Tribal marks and other physical alterations that are made at this time serve the dual purpose of identifying the adolescent boy or girl as a member of the group and also attracting members of the opposite sex, with the object of marriage.

In addition to puberty rites, the most important events in tribal life, among the Bantu as well as other East African peoples, are marriage and birth. Girls, even nowadays, usually marry in their early to middle teens. Boys may be somewhat older, as much depends on their being able to provide a *bridewealth,* and some young men now go to the towns to work for a few years in order to earn the necessary cash.

Almost all tribal marriages, whether arranged by the family or between the girl and boy with family approval, are sealed with the giving of the bridewealth. This transfer of property —usually livestock, grain, cloth, cooking pots, farming implements, or cash—is of more importance than the marriage ceremony itself, be it a tribal, Moslem, or Christian wedding. If the groom cannot produce the bridewealth, the couple may have to elope and will lose status in the tribe. To avoid this dilemma, a recognized marriage may take place, with the bridewealth being paid on the installment plan, a cow or a goat at a time. When divorce occurs, the wife's family must return the bridewealth or a portion of it. Divorce is fairly common in tribal society, but it probably would be much more widespread if not for the stabilizing influence of the bridewealth.

Often the members of the "extended family"—uncles, brothers, cousins, and other relations—pitch in to provide the bridewealth. In this way they gain some control of the newly married pair and their offspring. Africans who leave the tribal home area to get good jobs in the cities often complain that they are expected to share their income with dozens of quite distantly related family members. Ambitions sometimes are dimmed by this prospect. Of course, the East African institution of the extended family has its advantages, for it is always there to help in time of hardship.

The entanglements of the extended family are further com-

plicated by the fairly widespread practice of polygyny in East
Africa. It is estimated that a little over one third of the men
who marry take more than one wife at a time. Polygyny was
well established among the tribes before the introduction of the
Moslem religion by Arab traders. As Moslems, too, are permitted
to have several wives—usually up to four—this religion was
quite acceptable to many African tribal people. Today some
Africans who profess to be Christians carry on this practice,
and often the local churches tolerate it as preferable to losing
their parishioners.

Africans defend polygyny as a practical solution to the
problem of having more women than men in the population.
Each wife in a polygynous marriage lives in her own small hut
and has her own food supplies and cooking pots. Her children
live with her, but she is less burdened with the care of her
husband as this responsibility is shared among the wives. Also,
she does not have children in such rapid succession as does
the wife in the monogamous marriage and sometimes is able
to nurse each child for several years. The first wife has the most
authority, but all wives are supposed to be treated equally.
Jealousies and squabbles do arise but usually are buried soon
in the mutual need for child caring among the mothers, when
one is ill or overburdened, and in the general liking for the
social side of communal living.

Most East African tribes are patrilineal societies. The wife
goes to live on the homestead of her husband's family and
inheritance passes from the father to the sons. There are some
matrilineal societies such as that of the Luguru, a large Bantu
tribe that lives in eastern Tanzania. Among the Luguru, the
husband goes to live in the wife's family's household, and
inheritance rights are passed on through the mother. As the
Luguru live near the coast, the scene of early Arab settlements,

many have become Moslems and practice polygyny. It is difficult for polygynous marriages to exist in a matrilineal society, as the husband must travel from one homestead to another to visit his various wives and has no fixed abode of his own, so many Luguru have turned to patrilineal customs.

Children are of prime importance in a marriage, and the wife's inability to produce offspring is a frequent cause for divorce. Most tribes have fertility rites, and pregnant women must observe strict food and social taboos. Attempts to introduce birth control, because of East Africa's zooming population, usually are rejected fiercely. Such ideas are sometimes suspected of being a plot to reduce the number of Africans so that the country can be taken over by a foreign group or power. Girl children are valued almost as much as boys, for daughters bring the bridewealths that are needed in order to arrange

Adolescent Masai girls in beaded headbands and collars, wearing traditional garments of softened cattle hides

marriages for the sons. A polygynous father with many daughters may even use their bridewealths to get himself more wives.

The very essence of East African tribal life, among the Bantu as well as other indigenous peoples, is expressed in its music and dance. Religious ceremonies, births, marriages, deaths, harvest festivals, and the time of the full moon are all occasions for vigorous rhythmic dances accompanied by drums, gongs, rattles, piercing ululating shrieks, handclapping, and even wind and string instruments. The costumes worn on these occasions show the skill and inventiveness of tribal artisans in converting animal horns and bones, shells and hair, feathers and skins, into dazzling headdresses, garments, and body ornaments. Interesting examples are the ostrich-feather headdresses of the Masai and the Acholi, and the *aloket* headdress of the Turkana

Left: A Masai warrior in an ostrich-feather headdress
Right: A Turkana tribesman wearing the *aloket* headdress

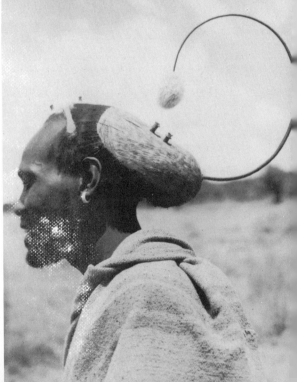

and Suk. The *aloket* is a loop of woven giraffe hair attached to a mud-plastered chignon at the back of the wearer's head.

Most objects made by tribal peoples, especially in the past, served useful purposes, even when they were articles of self-adornment such as the Masai maiden's patiently worked beaded headband or collar. The Masai warrior's buffalo-hide shield, the suedelike bark cloth and silken-smooth grass mats of the Baganda, the Turkana herdsman's carved wooden pillow, designed to preserve his elaborate headdress, are all examples of craftsmanship and artistry that have functioned as part of everyday life. Art for art's sake was an unknown concept. On the other hand, the carved animal figures and human statuettes of the Kamba woodcarvers of Kenya and of the Makonde carvers of coastal Tanzania are outgrowths of tribal arts that today are directed at tourists and the broad commercial market.

A Kamba woodcarver

East African religions nowadays show a blending of tribal beliefs and practices along with the Islam or Christianity that numbers of tribal peoples have accepted. In most pure tribal religions, there is a high god, a distant spiritual being who is responsible for the creation of the earth and all its creatures. The Bantu tribes of Tanzania have usually called this god Mulungu, the descendants of the Bantu peoples of the old Ankole, Bunyoro, and Toro kingdoms of Uganda call him Rukanga, while their Nilotic neighbors to the north—the Acholi and the Lango—call him Jok. This god is unapproachable, for few tribal peoples believe that a supreme being of such power and importance would involve himself in the everyday affairs of men. Further, they believe that god is good. Evil happenings such as drought, pestilence, disease, barrenness, and death are blamed on supernatural spirits that sometimes are identified as witches or sorcerers living within the tribe or as angry ancestor spirits.

In fact, the origin of most trouble-causing spirits is vague, but still they must be appeased. The methods include animal sacrifices, dances, food taboos, magic formulas, charms worn on the body, or exorcism rituals under the advice and direction of a tribal elder or a priest, healer, or diviner. Diviners also interpret dreams and visions and foretell the future. They may do so by throwing a set of bones on the ground and telling the meaning of the positions into which they have fallen, or by slaughtering a chicken or other animal and examining the internal organs. Chicken divination is very common. The shape, size, and color of the vital parts are a cue to future happenings or to a course of action to be taken.

In keeping with their view of the divine creator as a wholly good but uninvolved being, most tribal peoples believe that death was not brought on by god but by evil spirits. For this reason, houses in which death has occurred are shunned or even burned, and often the entire village must be cleansed by ritual. Usually a diviner is consulted to determine which supernatural spirits caused the death so that they can be eliminated or avoided.

Among most tribes the death wail is the wordless announcement by means of which this unhappy news is spread. Among the Nyamwezi, a Bantu people of Tanzania who live to the south of the Sukuma, the women raise the death moan at the bedside of the deceased, passing it on to the rest of the family, to neighbors, and even to passing strangers. Among almost all of East Africa's tribal peoples, realism and simplicity mark the final rites. In former times the bodies of the deceased usually were placed out in the bush and left for the jackals and hyenas. Now the custom is to remove the ornaments from the body and wrap it in a cloth. It then is buried in a grave covered with stones or thorns to keep predatory animals away.

For centuries the customs and traditions of East African tribal life served as a rock of stability in an uncertain natural environment. The influx of foreign peoples, beginning with the Asian traders of the tenth century, caused some tribal groups to cling all the more rigidly to their traditional life styles, while others bent more easily to the new persuasions. In the long run, however, all were to experience the disruptive influences that came with the mounting waves from abroad.

III
YEARS OF
EXPLOITATION

Two thousand years ago, when the first Bantu land migrations into East Africa were getting under way, vessels from Asia probably were already calling at East African shores. The first sailing ships had little difficulty in reaching these unexplored coastlands, for they were literally blown across the Indian Ocean by the favorable monsoon, a strong wind that comes from the northeast every year between November and March. In April, the wind turns back on itself, blowing the ships homeward until October.

By the tenth century, large numbers of Arab and Persian traders were sailing regularly out of the Persian Gulf, into the Arabian Sea, and across the Indian Ocean on the northeasterly monsoon. Their high-sided, tublike vessels, called dhows, were primarily designed for carrying cargo. The ships arrived in East

Africa laden with rugs and beads, cloth, metal, and glassware, as well as dates and camels. On the return voyage to Asia the dhows carried ivory, tortoise shell, and rhino horn, skins and hides, mangrove poles, and slaves.

These African exports were in strong demand in both Asia and Europe. Ivory, of course, was wanted for carvings while rhino horn, which is really composed of compacted hairlike

Arab dhows like those that first sailed from Asia to East Africa

matter rather than horn or bone, was sold in powdered form for its supposed aphrodisiac properties. (Although rhino horn is still in demand today, its value as an aphrodisiac is purely mythical.) The trade in African wildlife products was not limited to elephant tusks and rhino horns, and the tribal peoples who came in contact with the Arab trading caravans willingly slaughtered the plentiful game, using poisoned arrows, nets, and snares with cactus-fiber or wire nooses. Giraffes were destroyed for their tails, which were sold for fly whisks, ostriches for their feathers, used as hat plumes, fans, and feather boas; leopards and cheetahs were slain for their skins. While East Africans long had been killing game for food as well as for the horns, skins, and feathers used in their dress, ornamentation, and tribal ceremonies, the profit motive led to growing devastation of their wildlife.

The tenth-century influx of Arabs, Persians, and Indians into coastal East Africa resulted, of course, in the intermingling of Asians and Africans. Intermarriage between the two groups produced a people known as the Swahili, which means "coastal people." Swahili was also the name given to the new coastal language that developed. Based on Bantu language structure, Swahili included a great many Arabic, Persian, and Hindi words. Later Portuguese, Turkish, and English words were absorbed into the language. Swahili penetrated East Africa all the way to the shores of Lake Victoria and came to serve as a broad base of communication among African tribes of different ethnic families, as well as among Africans, Asians, and Europeans.

The Asians brought a variety of religions with them to East Africa. Mosques with pencil-slim minarets and ornate Hindu temples soon were scattered along the offshore islands and coastal trading settlements of what are today Kenya and Tan-

Opposite: The Swahili, a people of mixed Asian and African heritage

zania. In time, Islam, the Moslem faith, reached deep into the heart of Africa, where converts were made of many African tribal peoples.

One of the first coastal trading centers to be developed, in the 950's A.D., was Kilwa Kisiwani (Kilwa on the Island), south of where Dar es Salaam now is located. Soon the entire coastal region, between the modern countries of Somalia and Mozambique, was known as Zinj-el-barr, Arabic for "land of the blacks." The island of Zanzibar, which took its name from these very words, began to engage in a vigorous trading life by

Arab boys in *kanzus* and Moslem skullcaps at a mosque near Malindi

the thirteenth century. Other islands in this coral chain off what is today the Tanzanian coast—Pemba to the north of Zanzibar and Mafia to the south—developed along similar lines. In Kenya, the island of Lamu and the coastal towns of Malindi and Mombasa were also thriving ports for the Arab dhows by the thirteenth century.

Today the East African coastal towns are bustling commercial cities, but a fragment of the Asian past on the Kenyan coast is captured in the ruins of Gedi, which lie ten miles south of Malindi and today are preserved as a national park. Gedi,

The Tomb of the Fluted Pillar, a portion of the Gedi ruins near Malindi

The Portuguese-built Fort Jesus at Mombasa

which flourished between the thirteenth and seventeenth centuries, was an Arab port town typical of its period, although the
reason for its demise remains a mystery. The excavated portion
of the town reveals a great mosque, a palace, and a number of
wealthy merchants' houses, all built of coral stone. Household
and personal items ranging from Chinese porcelain bowls to
Venetian glass beads have been found in the crumbling masonry
of these onetime comfortable villas. However, the mud-and-
wattle huts of the majority of Gedi's inhabitants, along with
other impermanent structures, have vanished.

Possibly Gedi was a victim of the Arab and Portuguese
struggle for control of the East African coast. In 1498, on his
first voyage to India, Vasco da Gama called at Mombasa and
Malindi. For two hundred years subsequently, the Portuguese

carried on a sporadic effort to dominate the trade and political life of the coast. In 1593, they built Fort Jesus at Mombasa, its soaring stone walls rising from a coral ridge above the harbor. The fort changed hands a number of times over the years, but in 1698 Arabs from Oman, on the southeast coast of the Arabian peninsula, gained a strong foothold. Afterward, the Portuguese were forced back to the territory south of the Ruvuma River, which today serves as the border between Tanzania and Mozambique.

The moist, lush coastal islands appealed strongly to the Arab chieftains from the deserts of Oman. In 1824, the Omani ruler, Sultan Sayyid Said, built himself a palace on Zanzibar Island, on the site of the town of Zanzibar. In 1840, he officially transferred the capital of the Omani state from Muscat on the Arabian peninsula to the island, twenty-two miles off the coast of East Africa. When Sayyid Said died in 1856, Majid, his son by one of his seventy wives, became ruler. In 1861, under Sultan Majid, Zanzibar became an independent sultanate, its connection with Oman permanently severed.

The years 1830 to 1870 saw the peak of Zanzibar's prosperity, along with an alarming growth in the East African slave trade, most of which was dispatched through the island's slave markets and dhow harbor. Routes to the interior had been established long ago by the Arab slavers, who had brought out a small but steady supply of captives, mainly for sale as personal or household servants. The slavers were frequently aided in their activities by the local tribes such as the Nyamwezi, whose lands lay in the direct route of the caravans, just to the east of Lake Tanganyika. Under their warlord chieftain, the Nyamwezi raided weaker tribes for slaves and ivory, which they delivered to the Arabs in exchange for firearms.

The demand for slave labor increased with the growth of

plantation economies beginning in the latter half of the eighteenth century. Soon field workers were wanted for the clove and coconut-palm plantations on Zanzibar and the East African coast, as well as for sugar plantations on the island of Mauritius in the Indian Ocean, and for cotton and tobacco plantations in far-off America. The United States was one of the first Western countries to trade with Zanzibar. An American consulate was established on the island in 1837 to assist the commercial transactions of the ships that brought *merikani*, unbleached cotton cloth much in demand, and other manufactured goods that the masters of the merchant ships traded for slaves.

By 1840, about 40,000 slaves a year were being sold out of East Africa. They were marched hundreds of miles to the coast from as far away as Lake Tanganyika, Lake Nyasa, and the southern shore of Lake Victoria. Mothers and children were chained together by the neck, while the men often were made to serve as bearers, carrying elephant tusks or other heavy loads on their shoulders or heads. A common practice was to form the slaves into columns secured by a series of forked poles. Each captive had his head locked into the forked end by means of a wooden crossbar. The pole end rested on the shoulder of the man in front whose head was similarly encased. Many died before reaching the coast. At Bagamoyo, a small mainland port, the slaves embarked for Zanzibar, where they were exhibited at the slave market or marched about in the streets by slave masters calling out their wares. Those not sold for work on the island itself were packed into caves on the Zanzibar beach to await loading onto the dhows that would carry them away to Asian ports. Bagamoyo, the enslaved African's final point of contact with his native soil, is a Swahili name. It translates into the despairing words, "throw away your heart."

European powers—Great Britain, France, Germany—as well

Hoisting sail to an Arab sea chanty on a dhow
like those that once carried African slaves

as the United States, were involved in brisk trading activities at
Zanzibar by the beginning of the nineteenth century. In Britain
the outcry against the slave trade became so great that slavery
was abolished in 1807. But, despite agreements with the sultan
of Zanzibar, Britain found slavery very difficult to control in
the British-held territories of Asia. Some of Zanzibar's most
prosperous slave traders were, in fact, Indians and therefore
British subjects. In 1841, Great Britain established a consulate
on Zanzibar, one of its purposes being to oversee the enforce-
ment of an 1822 treaty with the sultan that outlawed the sale of

slaves to Christians but not to Moslems. Since there were in-
numerable ways to get around this law and the more severe
measures that followed as well, the Zanzibar slave trade continued to flourish well into the 1870's.

The antislavery issue, among others, began to draw the attention of European missionaries and explorers to Africa. The
Scotsman, David Livingstone, who first arrived in southern
Africa in 1841, was a missionary, medical doctor, abolitionist,
and explorer all rolled into one. He was followed by other
Europeans of similar callings and by groups with commercial
interests, frequently backed by their foreign governments. These
individuals and groups from the Western world brought the
first real shock waves of change to East Africa.

Like Livingstone, two German missionaries, Johann Reb-
mann and Johann Ludwig Krapf, had been sent to Africa by an
English church society in the early 1840's. When their reports
of seeing snow atop Mount Kenya and Mount Kilimanjaro
reached London in the late 1840's, a member of the Royal Geographic Society voiced strong disbelief, and the old controversy
as to the source of the Nile once again came up for discussion.
Could there be snowcapped mountains on the equator? If so,
did such mountains feed the Nile source? Was Ptolemy's sec-
ond-century map of the Lunae Montes based on fact or fantasy?
And what about the report of Herodotus, the Greek historian
who in the fifth century B.C. had sailed the Nile as far south as
the first cataract at Aswan and stated that the Nile rose from
two great fountains deep in the heart of Africa?

Then, in the mid-1850's, the famous slug map appeared.
Based on assorted reports by African tribal peoples, the hearsay
of Arab traders, and the fragmentary investigations of European missionaries, this map depicted a great inland sea lying

hundreds of miles from the East African coast and shaped in a curve like a giant slug with a thick body and a narrowing tail.

At this time the explorers Richard Francis Burton and John Hanning Speke, backed by the Royal Geographic Society of Great Britain, undertook their historic first expedition into East Africa. Their goal was to solve the mystery of the Nile source, to determine once and for all what rivers, lakes, or mountains gave birth to the mighty stream that had cradled one of the world's oldest civilizations and still flooded its banks each year, maintaining a fertile funnel of land in the midst of the Egyptian desert.

The route chosen by Burton and Speke was the historic route of the Arab traders. They sailed from India to the East African coast on the northeasterly monsoon, landed at Zanzibar, crossed to Bagamoyo on the mainland, and then traveled overland on foot to Ujiji on the shore of Lake Tanganyika, which they thought might be the source of the Nile. Their journey covered eight hundred miles and took them eight months, including a stopover of several weeks at the Arab trading village of Kazeh, now called Tabora, in central Tanzania. Hardships beset them at every turn. African bearers deserted, supplies were stolen, precious instruments were smashed or lost, their health was broken. Speke went temporarily blind, and Burton lost the use of his legs for months.

Yet no other route appeared possible at the time. To travel southward on the Nile from Egypt was extremely hazardous. There were six cataracts to be ascended between Aswan and Khartoum. And south of Khartoum was the fearful Sudd, a steamy jungle swamp through which the Nile meandered sluggishly, balked by great islands of floating vegetation. Land travel along the Nile was even more forbidding, due to the combination of desert, swamplands, and hostile peoples.

Once the two explorers reached Lake Tanganyika, in February, 1858, Speke began to have grave doubts that this body of water could be the Nile source or, in fact, was in any way connected with the great river. They learned, too, upon close questioning of the local tribes, that the slug map was inaccurate. The "inland sea," as it turned out, was actually three great lakes—Victoria, Tanganyika, and Nyasa—linked into one, with their borders and locations very roughly estimated.

Upon arriving back in Kazeh for a rest and recuperation stop, Speke determined to strike north to the great *nyanza* (lake) the local people had described. Leaving behind the somewhat indifferent Burton, who doubted the *nyanza* was likely to be the Nile source, Speke set out with a small party of African guides and bearers and reached the shore of the lake near the present site of Mwanza in August of 1858. Although he saw

The onetime site of Ripon Falls, now Owen Falls Dam

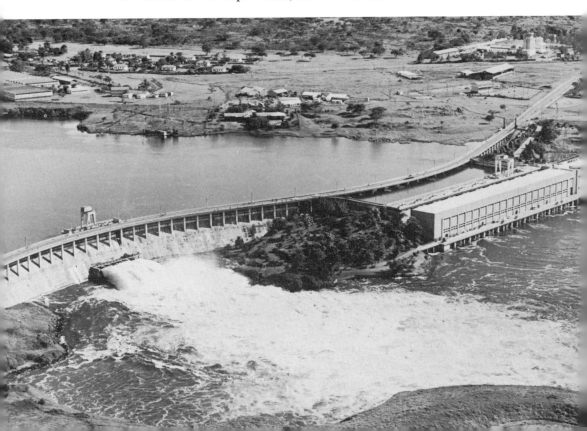

only a very small portion of the world's second largest lake on this visit, Speke sensed its greatness. Making further calculations from the lake's elevation and location, he declared it to be the source of the Nile and named it Victoria after Britain's queen.

Speke returned to East Africa under the sponsorship of the Royal Geographic Society in 1862, this time with James Augustus Grant as his coexplorer. He circled the western shore of Lake Victoria, visiting the Kingdom of Buganda, and then proceeded to the northern end of the lake where he viewed the outflow of water that directly fed the Nile River, which he named Ripon Falls after an officer of the Royal Geographic Society. Speke had no doubts at all that Victoria was the river's true source and the message he sent to the Royal Geographic Society in London said simply, "The Nile is settled."

But European investigation into East Africa was only beginning. In 1864, Samuel Baker, a wealthy and much-traveled Englishman, arrived at the Kingdom of Bunyoro in what is now western Uganda. The amazing Baker, traveling on his own funds and accompanied by his young wife, had sailed up the Nile by boat from Khartoum and managed, with some difficulty, to get through the Sudd. While in Bunyoro, the Bakers visited and named both Lake Albert (after Queen Victoria's consort, Prince Albert, who had died in 1861) and Murchison Falls (after Sir Roderick Murchison, a noted geologist and the president of the Royal Geographic Society).

Soon after the opening of the Suez Canal, in 1869, Baker took a high-ranking post with the government of Egypt, which was then under Turkish rule. His assignment was ostensibly to suppress the slave trade. In reality, Baker's project was to annex Bunyoro to Egypt, which already had the Sudan under its control. Baker's own government raised no opposition, for the Ot-

toman Empire of Turkey was tottering, and Britain had a growing interest in Egypt and the Sudan, as well as the Nile-source
region that lay to the south. Baker's campaign of 1872 to con-
quer the Kingdom of Bunyoro was a bloody one. There were
months of skirmishes during which villages were burned and
many Banyoro lost their lives. But Baker at last was forced to
retreat. This first attempt at outright takeover of an East African domain by a foreign power failed.

Meanwhile, in England, the Nile-source controversy continued to simmer. Speke had died in 1864, an apparent suicide
at the age of thirty-seven, with both Burton and the venerable
Doctor Livingstone still doubting that the Nile was born out of
Lake Victoria. Livingstone theorized that the river really origi-
nated in Lake Tanganyika, flowed out of it into Lake Albert,
and thus became the Albert Nile. In 1865, the Royal Geographic Society sent Livingstone to Africa on what was to be
his final journey. The British government contributed to the cost
of Livingstone's expedition, making his mission a semiofficial
one, but at the same time supplying no real support for the sup-
pression of the slave trade in which it publicly had professed
deep interest.

In 1866, Livingstone arrived in Zanzibar, where the sale of
slaves was still thriving. He soon set out for the interior following a route along the Ruvuma River. The next few years were a
time of weary wandering and heavy discouragement, during
which Livingstone was so little heard from that he was pre-
sumed lost. This disappearance prompted the famous "Livingstone search" of Henry Morton Stanley, a Welsh-born journal-
ist-adventurer who had gone to the United States as a ship's
cabin boy at the age of eighteen, had fought in the Civil War,
and now worked as a reporter for the New York *Herald*. If the
expedition to find Livingstone was something of a publicity

stunt, it was also a rough piece of adventuring, even for the thirty-year-old Stanley with his well-outfitted contingent of African porters, always led by a standard-bearer carrying the flag of the United States of America.

Stanley tracked Livingstone to Ujiji on the shore of Lake Tanganyika, where the two men met in the fall of 1871 and Stanley uttered the now-familiar words, "Doctor Livingstone, I presume." Like so many other dedicated people who have spent long years away from home, Livingstone did not really want to be "found." After some months together exploring the Lake Tanganyika shoreline, which yielded no trace of an outflowing stream, the two parted. Stanley went to England, while Livingstone groped his way deeper into central Africa, now believing that Lake Bangweulu, which lay to the south of Lake Tanganyika, would provide the stream that flowed into Lake Albert. Ill and exhausted, Livingstone died in the spring of 1873, in the vicinity of Lake Bangweulu, in what is today Zambia. He was farther away than ever from the true source of the Nile, but although he had failed in this endeavor, he had succeeded in another for, during his months with Stanley, Livingstone had imparted his missionary's zeal to his young companion.

By 1875 Stanley was back in Africa on a well-financed expedition. In addition to making thorough explorations by boat of both Lake Victoria and Lake Tanganyika, Stanley visited the court of Mutesa in the Kingdom of Buganda. Since Speke's visit thirteen years earlier, the kingdom had grown in size and its ruler had become sophisticated and adept at dealing commercially and politically with both the Zanzibar Arabs and the envoys of the Egyptians and the Sudanese. Islam had been introduced in Buganda, but at Stanley's urging Mutesa gave permission for Protestant missionaries to be sent from England. They were soon followed by a group of Roman Catholic missionaries from France. Mutesa himself professed to be a Moslem and so did not adopt either branch of the Christian faith, but he played them off against each other in a series of clever political moves, by means of which he guarded the independence of Buganda until his death in 1884.

However, under Mutesa's son and successor, Kabaka Mwanga, these plans miscarried, and internal religious strife became so severe that by 1894 Great Britain was in a position to establish a formal protectorate over Buganda. Two years later, in 1896, Bunyoro, Ankole, and Toro (the remaining kingdoms) were added to the British-controlled territory. Although Buganda was permitted to maintain a position of autonomy in the new protectorate, virtually all of what is today known as Uganda was in the hands of a foreign colonial power.

Upon leaving Mutesa's court, in 1875, Stanley completed his boat trip around Lake Victoria's shoreline and confirmed Speke's assertion that Ripon Falls was indeed the Nile overflow. Stanley also noted that the Kagera River, which flowed into Lake Victoria from the west, was a major inlet that could be considered the ultimate source of the Nile. Among geographers, some purists feel that the Kagera, which rises in what is today Rwanda, should be identified as the true source of the Nile.

After leaving the Nile-source region, in 1876, Stanley accomplished the almost incredible feat of crossing the African continent by sailing westward on the jungle-bordered Congo River and emerging on the shores of the Atlantic. In this operation, as in his encounters with Livingstone and with Mutesa, Stanley turned out to be an African empire builder for foreign governments. When Britain showed no interest in backing further exploration into the rich heart of Africa, Stanley approached King Leopold II of Belgium, who readily commissioned him to make treaties with the local chiefs. In this way, Stanley delivered the Congo, with its stores of ivory and rubber and its enormous agricultural potential, directly into the hands of a European monarch.

On the coast of East Africa, another empire builder, Doctor Karl Peters, was at work. Peters, founder of an organization called the Society for German Colonization, arrived in Zanzibar in 1884, carefully keeping his official status a secret from the authorities. He then crossed to the mainland where he proceeded to "buy" tracts of land from the local chiefs in return for trade goods and the promise of German "protection." As these African tribesmen did not have concepts of land ownership, as understood in Europe, nor any understanding of the risks of foreign protection, Peters' treaties clearly took advantage of a people from a different culture, as in the case of Stanley's treaties with the Congo chiefs. Nevertheless, Peters made his agreements stick, and in 1885 he got the German government's stamp of approval in the form of a land charter issued by Chancellor Bismarck. The new territory was dubbed German East Africa, and Peters became head of a politically influential commercial enterprise known as the German East Africa Company.

The sultan of Zanzibar, who had regarded the coastal region of the mainland as being under his control, immediately appealed to the British for help. By this time Britain had gained considerable influence on Zanzibar, mainly through its efforts to stop the slave trade and to build up other exports instead. Sultan Barghash, who had succeeded the dissolute Majid in 1870, cooperated with the British, and by 1876 the slave markets on the island were closed and the sea commerce in slaves had dwindled to a comparative trickle. Ivory, cloves, copra, coconut oil, and rice became Zanzibar's principal exports.

The British government solved the problem of the sultan's sphere of influence with the Anglo-German Agreement of 1886. Zanzibar received the offshore islands of Lamu, Pemba, and Mafia, plus a strip, ten miles deep, of a six-hundred-mile stretch of the coastal mainland. At the same time, Britain and Germany divided the rights to the mainland territory beyond the coastal strip, a vast tract reaching all the way to Lake Albert and Lake Tanganyika. The German half of the territory lay to the south and was taken out of the hands of the German East Africa Company in 1891 and put under the direct administration of the German government as a protectorate. German East Africa was known later as Tanganyika, and still later as Tanzania.

Britain kept the northern half of the East Africa territory for itself because its eye was on distant Uganda. Not only was

Thomson's Falls, named by the Kenya explorer Joseph Thomson in 1883

Uganda strategically located at the Nile source, it was a green and fertile land, particularly in the vicinity of Lake Victoria. German East Africa, on the other hand, was a vast upland of dry bush and plains except for its coastal strip. As the British explorers such as Burton and Speke had reported thirty years earlier, there was malaria at the coast, tsetse fly in the upcountry, and very little of exploitable value all the way from Dar es Salaam to Lake Tanganyika.

Kenya was of no particular interest to the British at the time of the Anglo-German Agreement, except as a means of access to Uganda. Kenya's central-highland country, which then was inhabited by the intimidating Masai, had not even been crossed successfully by a European until 1883, when the intrepid Scottish explorer, Joseph Thomson, marched from Mombasa to Lake Victoria. En route he gave his name to Thomson's Falls, a waterfall (and later a town) in central Kenya, and to the Thomson's gazelle, a breed now affectionately known as Tommies.

Between 1886 and 1895, Great Britain strengthened and formalized its position in East Africa. In 1887, the Imperial British East Africa Company, a counterpart of the German East Africa Company, was given a trading concession in Kenya and bought rights to the coastal strip from the sultan of Zanzibar. In 1890, I.B.E.A. Company rights were extended to Uganda, and under a second Anglo-German Agreement Britain clearly established its intention to control the territory of Uganda. Britain also arranged to have rights to the supposedly independent islands of Zanzibar and Pemba, while Germany was to have rights to Mafia, the smallest and most southerly of the three islands that lay off the coast of German East Africa. In return for yielding rights to the two larger islands, Germany received from Britain the island of Helgoland in the North Sea.

By 1895 the British government had taken control out of the hands of the I.B.E.A. Company, and Kenya was declared a British protectorate, along with Zanzibar and Pemba. The sultan was rendered powerless, and Zanzibar's coastal strip in German East Africa naturally fell to Germany. The British reinforced their hold on East Africa by making Kenya a colony in 1920. Uganda, on the other hand, remained a protectorate throughout the period of British rule.

In the space of only fifty years, from the 1840's to the 1890's, the free peoples of East Africa had come to be dominated by two European powers—Great Britain and Germany. From that time on, the single most important influence was that of the West. The impact of Western cultural values, religions, and political systems upon the tribes and native kingdoms of East Africa was to cause more turmoil and social upheaval than had all the centuries of slaving and trading at the hands of the Asian intruders.

IV
TANZANIA

The Germans made some attempts to develop their protectorate in East Africa. Starting in the 1890's they introduced the cultivation of coffee, sisal, and cotton, and they built rail lines connecting important agricultural centers with the coast. Dar es Salaam, the capital, was laid out as a German administration center. It had been developed under Sultan Majid of Zanzibar in the 1860's, and its narrow, twisted streets of balconied houses and galleried shop fronts bore the chaotic stamp of an Arab port town.

The principal conflict during the period of German rule was the Maji Maji Rebellion of 1905 to 1907, a widespread uprising of Africans that resulted from the oppressive practices of the *akidas,* Arab and Swahili governors appointed by the Germans to serve as local administrators.

Missionary schools and some government schools were established, and Europeans were invited to settle and farm the land. But the inhospitable landscape, tropical diseases, and high cash investment kept European planters away. On the eve of World War I, in 1914, only about 5000 Europeans—mostly Germans, some Greeks, Dutch, Scandinavians, and French—had established themselves in the protectorate. The wealth that was produced from the coffee, sisal, and cotton plantations was taken out of the country, providing few benefits for the Africans whose land and labor grew these crops. Yet African troops were required to help the Germans fight the British in World War I. The battles were fought on Tanganyikan soil and 250,000 Tanganyikan soldiers lost their lives. In addition, disruption of tribal life created a widespread famine, resulting in many more deaths.

In 1920, after Germany's defeat in World War I, the country's official name was changed to Tanganyika, and it was placed under British administration as a League of Nations mandate. Britain showed little interest in the economic development of the new territory. By 1925, the expelled German settlers were permitted to return. Greeks and a growing number of Indians made up the greatest part of the remaining non-African population.

Some 80,000 Tanganyikan troops served with the British in World War II, but the country itself was little affected by the war. However, as witnesses to two world conflicts originating in Europe in a space of twenty years, Tanganyikans along with other European-dominated Africans began to lose faith in the supposed good judgment and political wisdom of the foreign powers that governed them. In 1946, following the war, Tanganyika was named a United Nations trust territory, still under British administration. Britain's postwar attempt at the eco-

A United Nations mission visiting Tanganyika in 1960 when it was still a trust territory and Nyerere (center) was president of TANU

nomic redemption of Tanganyika, the Groundnut Scheme of the early 1950's, was a source of further disillusionment. The Scheme, a plan for Tanganyika to grow peanuts on a large scale for world markets, met with failure.

In 1954, Tanganyika's growing nationalist movement expressed itself in the formation of the Tanganyika African National Union. The founder and guiding spirit of TANU was Julius K. Nyerere, the son of a chief of the small Zanaki tribe from near Lake Victoria. Nyerere, a Christian, had attended Makerere University in Uganda and Edinburgh University in Scotland, had taught school, and was both a scholar and a political theorist. Although TANU was at first regarded as radical and dangerous by the British administrators, its leaders soon proved the organization capable of drawing wide support in Tanganyika. The United Nations strongly recommended independence for Tanganyika, and on December 9, 1961, after a year of self-government, this new status was achieved peacefully, with Nyerere as prime minister. A year later, on December 9, 1962, Tanganyika became a republic, with Nyerere as president.

There were several reasons why Tanganyika was the first of the three East African countries to become independent. One, of course, was the strong and decisive leadership of Nyerere himself. An important contributing factor was the lack of tribal rivalry or of any single dominant tribal group seeking national leadership. The Sukuma, the country's largest tribe, were well organized on the local level but never had expressed a strong voice in national political affairs. In part, this detachment was because the Sukuma lived near Lake Victoria, at a great distance from the capital in a country with poorly developed transportation and communication facilities. On the other hand, the

Dar es Salaam, founded by Arabs, developed by
Germans, celebrating Tanganyikan independence

Swahili language, which was spoken everywhere in Tanganyika, was an effective tool for unification. Another factor favorable to independence was the lack of a powerful, homogeneous
European-settler population. Tanganyika never had been a
profitable colonial possession for either Germany or Britain,
and after the disastrous Groundnut Scheme, with its accom-
panying loss of British investment, Britain was in general not
sorry to relinquish its responsibilities in that country.

Speaking on the occasion of *uhuru* (independence) in 1961,
Nyerere realistically observed that all Tanganyika had won so
far was political independence, "the political power to decide
what to do." The achievement of "economic independence," or
"real freedom," was still to come.

In the first ten years of independence, Mwalimu (teacher), as
Nyerere is called, stressed increasingly the concept of *ujamaa*.
This Swahili word can be translated as familyhood or brother-
hood, but actually it refers to the "extended family," as understood in the traditional tribal sense. *Ujamaa* operates on the national level and on the local level. In its broadest sense it means
working together for the national good. Mwalimu has made
vivid examples of those who would work against the national
welfare, such as a group of Dar es Salaam university students
who, after receiving a free college education from the government, balked at performing the required national service. He
also has kept a sharp eye out for profiteers, whether African or
non-African, who seek to amass great wealth at the expense of
the many poor.

Ujamaa, on the local level, became an official policy goal in
1967. The *ujamaa* village is a cooperative rural community
similar to the Israeli *kibbutz*. Ideally, its people farm the land
and also build their own homes, schools, hospitals, and other

facilities as a group effort. The keynote, as in the extended-family relationship, is the responsibility of each individual to the group. At present about 11 percent of Tanzania's population is living in *ujamaa* villages. There are also state farms, operated directly by the government, to help increase agricultural production.

A major political event since independence has been the merger with the island of Zanzibar, which won independence from Britain in December, 1963. A month later, in January, 1964, a revolution took place on the 640-mile-square island, unseating the sultan, who, descended from the Omani, represented the traditionally powerful Arab minority on Zanzibar and Pemba. The new government was under the leadership of the Afro-Shirazi Party, made up of Africans and Shirazis, descendants of very early settlers from Shiraz in southern Persia. Early in 1964, a People's Republic of Zanzibar was proclaimed, with party head Sheik Abeid Karume as president. On Union Day, April 26, 1964, Tanganyika and Zanzibar agreed to form the United Republic of Tanganyika and Zanzibar, with Nyerere as president and Karume serving as president of Zanzibar and first vice president of the United Republic. In October, 1964, the country's unwieldy name was changed to the United Republic of Tanzania (pronounced Tan-zan-ee'-yah).

The island-mainland relationship has not always been an easy one. In addition to the differences in historical background, economic development, and population makeup, the new Zanzibar government swung far to the left in 1964, seizing and nationalizing the Arab-owned clove plantations and the Indian-owned import-export businesses with no compensation to their owners, ousting most Europeans, and bringing in technical advisers from Communist China, the Soviet Union, and East Germany.

By the early 1970's, however, Karume was steering an un-focused political course and ruling Zanzibar in a capricious, singlehanded fashion. Many considered him as despotic as some of the Arab sultans whose rule he had overthrown. In April, 1972, Karume was assassinated at Afro-Shirazi party headquarters by a group of Zanzibar gunmen believed to have had personal or political motives, leaving the course of affairs in Zanzibar in a state of confusion.

On the Tanzania mainland, political and economic strides to-ward socialism have been made in an orderly fashion. Since 1965, TANU has been the only legal political party in Tan-zania. Mwalimu Nyerere defends his "one-party democracy" as being less wasteful of resources and still offering a choice of candidates in national elections, although all such individuals must be approved by TANU. He has stated that the "Westmin-ster (British) model" of parliamentary democracy is a luxury and a danger in a developing country with masses of illiterate people who are unable to weigh important issues. If the people do want change, Nyerere asserts, they can express these wishes through TANU, as the party is structured so that it can act against an unpopular government.

Tanzania, the largest of the three East African countries with an area of 362,000 square miles, today has a population of over 13 million. The overwhelming majority—about 99 percent—of its people are Africans, principally of Bantu origin. Indians, Pakistanis, Arabs, and a very few Europeans and Americans make up the remaining one percent. Since *uhuru*, Africaniza-tion—the employment of Africans in all types of jobs and busi-nesses and on all levels—has been a long-term goal of the ad-ministration. A first step, however, was the leveling out of the pay scales, for under the colonial administration an African worker received less than an Asian worker in the same job, and an Asian, in turn, received less than his European coworker.

In the area of public service President Nyerere, in the early days of *uhuru*, supported the appointment of Africans, even though poorly qualified, to high government posts. Some, he later admitted, failed to do their jobs properly and had to be replaced. But he felt that African self-confidence had to be built up by proving to his people that "being an African did not have to mean being a junior official." After 1964, with lessons learned and a high degree of African pride gained, the Tanzania government abandoned racialism in the selection of job applicants and has stressed the importance of skills. President Nyerere's policy is: "Every citizen has the right to be considered on his or her merits, regardless of race, religion, or sex."

Asians traditionally have occupied roles in trade and commerce and in the professions of teaching, medicine, and law in East Africa. Africanization in Tanzania has proceeded most slowly in these special areas, as there have not been enough trained people to step into their places. Today Tanzania has 80,000 Asians, only a quarter of whom chose to become African citizens at independence. Yet President Nyerere does not contemplate repressive moves against them. He feels that race prejudice toward any group in Tanzania would be inconsistent with his country's condemnation of present-day racist policies in South Africa, Rhodesia, and the Portuguese colonial possessions in Africa.

Similarly, Nyerere states that religious prejudice has no place in Tanzania, which is about 30 percent Moslem, 25 percent Christian, and the rest adherents of tribal religions.

Swahili is today the official language of Tanzania and is widely spoken among the people. English, too, was an official tongue, but it now is regarded as being too strongly associated

A Tanzanian Moslem woman in a *boui-boui,* the Moslem
coverall garment, at a marketplace in Dar es Salaam

with colonialism and with Western capitalism to hold official
status in an emerging African socialist country. Swahili is the
language of instruction in the primary schools, but English is
taught as a subject, usually beginning in third grade. As most
higher-school textbooks are in English, that language still is
used in the secondary schools and on the university level, and it
also is used in commerce. Tanzania has no television, but the
government-controlled radio reaches about one third of the population, broadcasting largely in Swahili.

Only about 5 percent of Tanzania's population lives in cities
and towns. Dar es Salaam, which means "haven of peace" in
Arabic, is the capital and largest city with about 300,000 in-

habitants. Tanga, a coastal railhead and center for the sisal-producing region, is the second largest mainland town with about 60,000 people. It is followed by Mwanza, on the southern shore of Lake Victoria, and by Arusha and Moshi, business and agricultural centers on the fertile slopes of Mount Meru and Mount Kilimanjaro.

The town of Moshi with Mount Kilimanjaro in the background

Due to low rainfall, tsetse-fly infestation, lack of irrigation facilities, and other agricultural drawbacks, only about 10 percent of Tanzania's land area is presently under cultivation. The large rural population is unevenly distributed around the country. In the rich Chagga farmlands on the slopes of Mount Kilimanjaro, there is a population density of 800 persons per square mile; in the semidesert regions there are as few as 3. President Nyerere is the first to admit that agricultural methods have not improved greatly in the first ten years since *uhuru* and that only a few state farms and advanced *ujamaa* villages have motorized farming equipment. Most farmers do not even use ox plows but work with hoes and other hand tools to produce the maize, millet, wheat, cassavas, and beans for their daily needs, as well as the crops grown for export, which are produced on small farms as well as large ones. Mwalimu stresses that the farm population must not wait for agricultural specialists with certificates and degrees to tell them about new planting methods, seeds, and equipment, but must become self-reliant and help themselves by learning on the job and most of all by forming *ujamaa* villages. In this way, at least, trained agricultural field workers can reach large segments of the rural population at one time.

The export of coffee, cotton, and sisal now makes up about 50 percent of mainland Tanzania's foreign earnings, while Zanzibar and Pemba produce 80 percent of the world's supply of cloves. Mainland industries are largely geared to the processing of agricultural products—cotton ginning, coffee curing, sisal decortication. Other industries process tea, tobacco, pyrethrum (a plant whose flowers are made into an insecticide), cashew nuts, and oilseeds for export. Sugar is grown and refined in Tanzania but mainly for domestic consumption. Breweries, textile mills, flour mills, and an oil refinery supply the domestic

market only, as do the local factories that produce shoes, cement, cigarettes, paper, tin cans, and matches. Mwalimu does not consider the industrial development impressive, but it is certainly a great improvement over 1961, when Tanzanians found themselves having to spend precious foreign exchange for textiles woven abroad from the very cotton they themselves had grown.

The most important single step toward socialism, economically, was the Arusha Declaration of February 5, 1967, by means of which all of mainland Tanzania's banks and insurance companies were nationalized. A year earlier, in 1966, Tanzania withdrew from the East African Currency Board, created during colonial rule, and issued a Tanzanian currency to replace the East African shillings that had served for the three countries since before independence. The exchange rate of the new Tanzanian shilling was fourteen cents in United States money, or seven shillings to one dollar.

The Arusha Declaration also nationalized rice and flour mills, other large food-processing industries, large plantations and farming estates, eight large import-export and wholesale businesses, and subsequently many smaller businesses such as the shoe companies and cement factories that produced exclusively for the domestic market. Compensation was paid to the previous private owners.

Land, public utilities, transportation, and mineral deposits, such as the Williamson Diamond Mine at Shinyanga developed by a Canadian geologist in 1940, were already government-controlled by 1967. But despite the Arusha Declaration, Nyerere, with his characteristic streak of practicality, has continued to invite foreign investment into Tanzania, provided investors cooperate with the government and substantial benefits are distributed within the country as a result of profits earned.

Opposite: Drilling on the site of a United Nations irrigation
project to improve agricultural production in Tanzania

A growing source of national income today are Tanzania's wildlife domains, the national parks and game reserves through which tourism has grown from 10,000 visitors in 1966 to about 90,000 in 1972. At independence, Tanzania had only one national park where wild animals could be protected effectively from the ravages of poachers, meat-hungry tribesmen, sportsmen, and trophy hunters. Although colonial authorities took a dim view in 1961 of independent Tanganyika's ability to set aside additional protected natural habitats, Tanzania now has fourteen parks and game reserves where visitors with cameras rather than guns can view the country's enormous concentration of exceptional animal life.

Serengeti National Park, the oldest and largest protected wildlife area in Tanzania, occupies about 5000 square miles in the northern part of the country. Its territory extends to the Kenya border in the north and Lake Victoria in the west, and it is made up largely of vast short-grass and long-grass plains. The former are studded with peculiar islands, of huge, bulbous rock outcroppings known as *kopjes* (little heads), where sufficient moisture accumulates to support the growth of trees and thick vegetation.

The Serengeti plains first were visited by Europeans in the 1890's and soon became a favorite hunting ground for German and British sportsmen. By the 1920's, the Serengeti lions, which were regarded by many as vermin at that time, were being decimated by the growing number of hunting safaris. The pleas of conservationists went unheeded, for in those days East Africa's territory seemed endless and its resources limitless. Ecology, the science of nature's careful balance of relationships between living things and their environment, was an unfamiliar word.

Although the Serengeti was given national park status in 1951, controls were weak, and there were constant threats to

cut away sections of the park territory. In the late 1950's, Bernhard Grzimek, the director of Germany's Frankfurt Zoo, and
his son Michael undertook a study of the Serengeti with the
aim of bringing both the plight and the habits of its animal
population to the public's attention. The Grzimek study included the overwhelming task of taking a census of the Serengeti wildlife as well as tracing the patterns of migration within
the park and adjacent areas. Basing themselves in the Serengeti
and the Ngorongoro Crater area to the east of it, the Grzimeks
made daily flights in a small plane to track and count the animals. Their important achievement, which helped in setting the
park's present borders, cost the life of Michael Grzimek, who
was killed when his plane crashed while out alone on a track-
ing mission. The freak accident was caused by a vulture flying
into the wing of the plane. Michael Grzimek is buried on the
rim of Ngorongoro Crater, not far from where he died. The in-
scription on his gravestone reads simply: "He gave all he pos-
sessed, including his life, for the wild animals of Africa."

One of the most dramatic features of the Serengeti docu-
mented by the Grzimeks is the annual migration of some
400,000 wildebeest from the centrally located short-grass country to the northern and western reaches of the park, where
there is permanent water. Five months later, when the rains
come, the animals trek back again to the short-grass area. These
mass migrations are dictated by local weather conditions and
vary slightly from year to year. They usually last three days.
During November to May, the months of the single long rainy
season in north central Tanzania, the wildebeest share the
short-grass plains of the Serengeti with 200,000 zebra and well
over half a million gazelle, as well as ostrich, giraffe, hartebeest, topi, and of course lion, leopard, cheetah, and other pred-
ators and scavengers.

A tourist-revenue attraction second only to Serengeti National Park is the Ngorongoro Conservation Area, which includes the remarkable geological phenomenon of Ngorongoro Crater. The crater is more correctly described as a caldera, for it consists of a broad, bowl-shaped depression that is really a cross section of the volcanic mountain itself. This depression, which resulted from volcanic eruption, measures many times the diameter of the collapsed volcanic cone and so is much larger than an ordinary crater. The floor of Ngorongoro is between 10 and 12 miles in diameter and has a total area of 102 square miles. The crater floor lies at 5500 feet, while the steep-sided rim rises 2000 feet to a forested ridge with an elevation of 7500 feet.

The bowl of Ngorongoro supports an array of wildlife, most

A lion in Ngorongoro Crater, with crater wall in background

of which does not migrate from the area because of the encir-
cling crater walls. The crater floor offers level grasslands for
plains animals, large ponds for flamingos and other water birds,
green thickets fed by underground streams that are the lair of
lions, and even small rounded hills. Elephant and buffalo frequent the wooded ridge country of the crater walls. Many
Masai live in the crater, for its great bowl receives more rainfall than the surrounding grasslands and makes better pasturage
for their herds.

Despite the advances made in the years since *uhuru*, Tanzania still has a long way to go. Its lack of favorable mineral or
agricultural resources combined with a generally indifferent 70-
year-long colonial administration have kept it well behind its
East African neighbors in terms of per capita income (about
$60 a year), life expectancy (38 years), and literacy (15 per-
cent).

President Nyerere has come up with a realistic outlook concerning education. Most postcolonial leaders have felt that
higher education for as many as possible was the key to national development. Nyerere has no such illusions. He is anxious to see the government provide free primary education for
all children, but he recognizes that "for the foreseeable future,
the majority of our primary school pupils will not go to secondary school, and the majority of our secondary school pupils will
not go to university." He is not antieducation, but he does realize the folly of "education for education's sake" at public expense in Tanzania and the futility of schooling youth for vague
or nonexistent urban jobs when the bulk of Tanzania's man-
power is wanted on the rural level and in the development of
ujamaa villages.

A first step at the time of independence was the integration of most religious and all racially segregated schools into a single government system. Tanzania now spends 20 percent of its budget on education, but primary schools are not free as yet and parents must pay modest fees. Children start primary school at age seven or eight and graduate after seven years, at which time most are expected to become useful and progressive workers.

While about 52 percent of Tanzania's children attend primary school, only about 2 percent attend secondary school. Since 1964, no fees have been charged on the secondary level. The University of Dar es Salaam was founded in 1961, shortly before independence, and is the youngest of the three East African universities, which together make up the University of East Africa. It began as a law faculty with only 14 students (an attempt to train African judges for the about-to-be-independent country). The Dar es Salaam Medical School, founded in 1963, became part of the university in 1968 and now accepts 30 to 40 students a year. University students are given government scholarships and pay no fees. At independence, Tanzania had a total of only 194 students attending the various colleges of the University of East Africa; today it has over 2000.

Health problems long have plagued Tanzania: malaria and sleeping sickness, malnutrition, tuberculosis, leprosy, parasitic diseases, polio, typhoid, smallpox, and venereal disease. Since *uhuru* there has been an improvement in nutritional problems that resulted from protein deficiency, as dairying has been stressed in rural areas and stock-raising tribes have been encouraged to market more of their meat animals. About 60 percent of the population now is protected against smallpox as the result of a vaccination campaign that got under way in 1968. Licensed doctors, even non-African ones, are still far too few, and hospitals are concentrated in the urban areas, but health

A health clinic in eastern Tanzania established
with the help of the United Nations Children's Fund

posts are being established in *ujamaa* villages with the prospect
of developing into well-equipped rural health centers.

Prenatal care is now available to about two thirds of Tanzania's mothers-to-be, twice as many as received it in 1961.
Adult education courses are provided for women in matters of
child care, health, hygiene, and nutrition. Women are encouraged to develop careers as nurses, social-service workers,
and even outside the traditional women's "helping" professions. Four women were elected to the National Assembly,
Tanzania's one-house legislature, in 1965, and in July, 1972,

Tanzania hosted the first All Africa Women's Conference in Dar es Salaam.

In its step-by-step development toward African socialism, Tanzania has made new friendships and acquired new trading partners among foreign nations. Relations with Great Britain, although strained at times, remain cordial, and there is substantial trade between Tanzania and the other Commonwealth countries, as well as with the United States, Japan, India, and the European Common Market countries. But the most significant association of the late 1960's was that of Tanzania and the People's Republic of China.

A major example of Chinese aid to Tanzania is the building of the Tanzam (Tanzania-Zambia) railway, scheduled for completion in the mid-1970's. This rail line gives inland Zambia a direct outlet to the coast through the friendly neighboring state of Tanzania and benefits Tanzania as well. President Nyerere resents insinuations that Tanzania is becoming an African satellite of Communist China and firmly states, "We shall never agree to be puppets, tools, or stooges of other people or of any other nation."

Tanzania professes a policy of nonalignment in world affairs. It recognizes the state of Israel while deploring United States involvement in Vietnam. "One thing, however, on which we have never pretended to be nonaligned," Mwalimu asserts, "is the liberation of all of Africa." Tanzania violently opposes the Portuguese regime in neighboring Mozambique as well as elsewhere in Africa, and the white-minority rule in South Africa and Rhodesia. Dar es Salaam long has had the reputation of being a center for revolutionary groups concerned with the overthrow of colonialism and neocolonialism in Africa.

As for other bordering states, there have been some problems

with Malawi due to its friendship with the South African regime. Also, tensions are growing with Uganda following the
coup that unseated its president, A. Milton Obote, in January,
1971, sending him to Tanzania for sanctuary. Relations with
Kenya have remained satisfactory.

Looking back on Independence Day ten years later, from the
vantage point of 1971, Nyerere told his people, "What we won
was the right to begin work—and nothing more. Now we have
achieved our Uhuru; we have defined and accepted the kind of
Tanzania we want to build and live in." The future course he
wants the country to pursue is that of *uhuru na kazi*—freedom
and work.

V
UGANDA

Uganda, the "cradle of the Nile," is surely East Africa's greenest and most pleasant land. From early Bantu times, the fertile soil, ample rainfall, and balmy climate of most of the southern half of the country fostered a leisure society that led to a more sophisticated form of tribal life. Around the fifteenth century kingdoms developed, and by the middle of the nineteenth century the five small monarchies of Busoga, Buganda, Bunyoro, Toro, and Ankole stretched from the northern and western shores of Lake Victoria to the lakes and valleys of the Western Rift.

After the British takeover of the four existing kingdoms in 1896 (Busoga, by that time no longer centrally organized, was not considered a kingdom), Buganda played a leading role in preserving Ugandan autonomy despite foreign control. In fact,

throughout the colonial era, it was the power of the local kingdoms that helped to maintain Uganda's status as a protectorate,
while the more tightly administered Kenya, which was directly
under British rule, was destined to become a colony.

The rulers of the four kingdoms did not submit readily to the
British administration. In 1897, Kabaka Mwanga of Buganda
led an unsuccessful revolt. He was replaced by his young son,
Daudi Chwa, whose early rule was carried out under three re-
gents. In 1899, after attempts to regain the throne, Mwanga
was captured by the British and deported to the distant islands
of the Seychelles in the Indian Ocean, where he died in 1903.
A fellow deportee was Kabarega, king of Bunyoro, who also
had rebelled against the British. Although the kingdoms of
Buganda and Bunyoro had been traditional enemies for genera-
tions, their rulers were at last joined in exile, in bitter opposition to foreign domination.

To establish a more peaceful understanding, the British
offered the Buganda Agreement of 1900. By its terms, Britain
recognized the authority of the *kabaka* and of the *lukiko*, Buganda's traditional council of chiefs and its lawmaking body. It
also recognized the legality of the land-tenure system that had
operated in Buganda in the past, and therefore the British authorities did not encourage European planters to settle in
Uganda as they did in Kenya. In 1904, the British introduced
cotton growing. Over two tons of seed were distributed to
Ganda (a shortening of the word *Baganda*) farmers by Britain's Church Missionary Society, which also gave instruction in
the cultivation of the new market crop. Soon a peasant economy of growing prosperity was established, for cotton and
coffee, an indigenous shrub in Uganda, were destined to become the country's major exports.

In 1896, the same year it established its formal protectorate

over Uganda, Britain undertook the construction of the railway
from Mombasa, on the Kenya coast, all the way to Lake Victoria. Building the eight-hundred-mile rail line meant breaking
ground through a wilderness of plains and forests, swamplands
and mountains, including the great Rift escarpment in Kenya,
where the elevation rose to 9000 feet. The main purpose of the
railroad was to transport land-bound Uganda's agricultural
wealth to the Indian Ocean for shipment to world ports. At the
same time, machinery and manufactured goods could be trans-
ported inland for the development of the country. To work on
the building of the railway, the British imported large numbers
of Indian laborers, many of whom remained in East Africa, settling in both Kenya and Uganda. British enterprise on behalf of
its promising new protectorate also led to a water-transport system for Lake Victoria and to the building of a network of interior roads, giving Uganda the best road system in East Africa
today.

After the death of Daudi Chwa in 1939, his son Edward
Fredrick Mutesa took the Buganda throne as Kabaka Mutesa
II, and Uganda's "state within a state" continued to function, although with somewhat more interference from the British administration than before World War I. The first serious stirrings
of the "Buganda issue" grew evident in the years following
World War II.

In 1948, the British established the East African High Commission, its purpose being to coordinate services such as transportation, telecommunications, health, and agricultural projects
for the three countries under British administration. Buganda
voiced opposition to the EAHC (which went into operation
nonetheless), fearing that any steps leading to closer union with
Kenya and Tanganyika would result in a loss of status and
authority for Buganda. While the kingdom still maintained its

autonomy within Uganda, it clearly did not have the support of all Ugandans within the national borders.

This conflict became even more evident in the early 1950's, when the British began to try to develop a unitary state in Uganda. Through this effort, a nationalist movement made up of non-Ganda peoples, such as the Acholi, Lango, Banyoro, Batoro, and Ankole, began to emerge. Soon the local Ganda chiefs began to riot and Mutesa II, refusing to put down the rioting, was exiled to England in 1953. However, unable to restore calm with the Kabaka in exile, the British permitted him to return to the Bugandan throne in 1955. King Freddie, as the monarch was called affectionately, pledged loyalty to Britain in return for British guarantees that his rights as a constitutional ruler would continue to be recognized.

As the independence movement in East Africa gathered strength in the late 1950's, Buganda led the struggle for Uganda, with the hope of being able to extend its influence in the newly independent state. However, when Uganda's independence was achieved on October 9, 1962, concessions had to be made to the non-Ganda tribal peoples. Mutesa II continued as ruler of Buganda while Apolo Milton Obote, who had been elected to the recently formed national legislative council from the district of the Lango tribe, became prime minister.

Uganda's progress since independence has been exceptionally difficult. Its problems have stemmed not from extreme poverty, indifference, and neglect during the colonial era, as in the case of Tanzania, but from intense tribalism. Having been the most powerful of the Ugandan kingdoms in precolonial times, Buganda sought from the late 1800's to dominate the non-Bantu peoples of the north, who had been incorporated into the Uganda protectorate by Great Britain for political reasons.

Kampala, Uganda's capital city, originally
the site of the capital of Buganda

(The British-formed Uganda encompassed the strategically located Nile source.) Here was a perfect example of a Western
nation trying to impose the idea of "nationhood," or political
unity, upon an African territory in which tribal units had traditionally served as political entities. Not surprisingly, this attempt at restructuring African society failed to work smoothly
and caused considerable discontent and hardship among African peoples.

In October, 1963, a year after independence, Mutesa II was
elected first president of Uganda by the national parliament,
but his office was given limited powers. Real authority rested

with Prime Minister Obote, who continued to work for national unity and a strong centralized government. The political struggle between Buganda and the nationalist forces continued until 1966, when Obote suspended the constitution of 1962, abolished the federal system through which Buganda's autonomy had been maintained, and unseated President Mutesa, who fled to England.

A 1966 interim constitution went into effect, giving the presidential office strong powers, and Obote took over the presidency himself. Under President Obote's new constitution of 1967, the traditional kingdoms and their hereditary rulers were abolished, the country was declared a republic, and the Uganda People's Congress, made up mainly of non-Ganda peoples, was declared the official political party, with all opposition parties outlawed.

The former Kabaka was not to return to power. In 1969, Mutesa II died in London. Soon afterward, an assassination attempt was made on Obote, who was considered by the Ganda people to have usurped Mutesa's office. The politically influential Ganda make up about 20 percent of the population and live mainly in and around the capital of Kampala, the traditional seat of the old Bugandan kings.

Obote's unpopularity grew when, in 1969, he promulgated his Common Man's Charter, believed by some to be a step toward the creation of a socialist state similar to that of Tanzania. His so-called "move to the left" was unwelcome to many Ugandans. Later, in mid-1970, Obote spoke of nationalizing Uganda's financial and business enterprises, despite the opposition of businessmen and the large, conservative Army officer element. Although many people doubted the sincerity of Obote's leftist intentions, they were further alienated by the favoritism he showed toward members of his own Lango tribe and the neighboring Acholi people, with whom he attempted to pack parliament as well as the army and his personal bodyguard.

In January, 1971, while President Obote was out of the country attending a Commonwealth Prime Ministers' Conference in Singapore, he was overthrown in a military coup by General Idi Amin Dada, chief of Uganda's armed forces since 1966 and a former close associate of Obote. Amin, a member of the northern Kakwa tribe (from the West Nile dictrict), had been courting the favor of the Ganda people. Although he declared after the takeover that Uganda would remain a republic and there would be no return to the kingdoms of old, he did keep his promise to bring home the body of King Mutesa II and, in April, 1971, gave him a state funeral with burial in the royal Kasubi Tombs on a Kampala hilltop. Amin stated that "free and fair general elections" would take place in Uganda as soon as possible. There had been no national election since 1962. Obote did not return to Uganda after the coup but proceeded directly to Tanzania, where he took refuge. President Nyerere, sympathizing with Obote's cause, refused to recognize the Amin government in Uganda.

In 1972, President Amin's regime was marked by two major policy moves in which Uganda's seething internal problems exploded, reaching well beyond its borders. In March, President Amin expelled the Israeli military, business, and technical advisers who had been in Uganda for a number of years and broke off diplomatic relations with Israel. His main reason appeared to be the offer of considerable financial aid from oil-rich Libya, a North African Moslem nation hostile to Israel. President Amin is himself a Moslem, but more important, observers felt, was Uganda's need for funds in view of the high military expenditures of recent years. Uganda's spending on its army and air force was believed to have quadrupled between 1969 and

1971 alone. Many of Uganda's economic difficulties also may be traced to years of mismanagement during the Obote regime.

An even more abrupt move on Amin's part was his announcement in August, 1972, that all Ugandan Asians holding British passports—an estimated 50,000 people, mainly of Indian origin —would have to leave Uganda within ninety days. Some weeks later it appeared that many of the additional 23,000 Asians who had chosen Ugandan citizenship at the time of independence also would be expelled. President Amin's action apparently was aimed at accomplishing "overnight Africanization" in Uganda, but it raised questions concerning, among other matters, Uganda's economy.

While Asians never have been thoroughly accepted in East Africa because of their higher economic status and their social

Asians and Africans studying together at a Kampala technical school prior to the expulsion of most Ugandan Asians

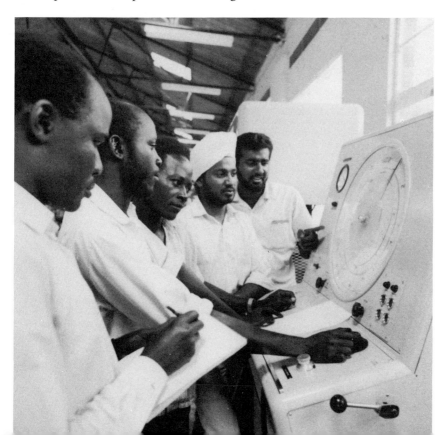

and religious clannishness, Uganda's Asian businessmen have been its principal taxpayers and employers. In mid-1972, Asians made up less than 1 percent of Uganda's population—about 80,000 in a country of 10 million. Yet they controlled 80 percent of Uganda's commerce and trade, and they constituted 75 percent of the country's doctors, lawyers, and teachers. Asian economic power was a sore point with African Ugandans, who felt that the gains of independence were incomplete in view of the continuing economic control of non-Africans.

Vestiges of the "totem pole" society of colonial days were still all too evident in Uganda in 1972, ten years after independence. Most of the British, who had occupied the top social positions, had departed, but the Asian still held his ascendancy over the African. He drove a Mercedes-Benz on Uganda's British-paved roads, while the African trudged along the side of the road breathing dust and exhaust fumes. Ugandan resort hotels and better restaurants were frequented by foreign tourists and by Uganda's Indian residents, seldom by Africans. Indians flew in the planes and rode in the first-class carriages of the railway trains. Well-to-do Indian families sent their children abroad to India for schooling, to Europe for university educations and professional degrees. Of course, many of Uganda's Asians were small shopkeepers with humble incomes, but compared to most Africans they seemed well off.

When President Amin's expulsion order came, it was in one respect a long-delayed reaction to the effects of British colonialism. In addition to having brought large numbers of Indians to East Africa for the building of the Kenya-Uganda railway, Britain, in the early years of the protectorate, had encouraged Indians to play the role of middlemen in the Ugandan economy, especially in the retail trade and in the marketing of cotton. As a result, there had been anti-Asian riots in Uganda in the 1940's and 1950's. It was not surprising, therefore, that the president's order seemed intended to make the British suffer as well as the Asian deportees. The fleeing British-passport holders, who were required to sell their Ugandan businesses on short notice to Africans only, had nowhere else to go but Great Britain, swelling that country's Asian population severely and intensifying the already troublesome racial problem there.

In making such an abrupt move to oust the country's Asians, many observers felt that President Amin was using the highly charged emotional appeal of this ready-made situation to increase his personal popularity and to divert the attention of Ugandans from other national problems. One unanswered question was how President Amin's racist action could be justified by Ugandans who, along with other East Africans, condemn racism elsewhere in Africa and throughout the world.

While Asians have monopolized the business sector of Uganda's economy, agriculture has remained primarily in the hands of Africans and is the means of livelihood for over 90 percent of the population. Small farmers living on homesteads surrounded by their cultivated fields raise bananas, grains, legumes, sweet potatoes, and cassavas for their own use, as well as the cash crops of cotton and coffee, which today make up 90 percent of Uganda's exports. Tea, a more recently introduced cash crop, and sugar are more often grown on large plantations. In an extension of his drive to make Uganda Africa's "first genuinely black" state, President Amin nationalized the British-owned tea plantations early in 1973 and ordered pay cuts for all British personnel in Uganda.

Although it is the smallest of the East African nations, with an area of about 91,000 square miles (16,000 square miles of it water), Uganda has the largest percentage of productive land:

Bananas being weighed for market in Uganda

78 percent. However, only about 25 percent is in agricultural use at any one time. Cattle are raised, including the famous Ankole longhorns. The Uganda Development Corporation, a government economic agency, currently is sponsoring large-scale cattle-ranching projects in order to develop a beef and dairy livestock industry and help diversify the country's exports. At present, Uganda must import half of its dairy products from neighboring Kenya. Fishing also is being expanded in Uganda, especially on Lake Victoria. The catch is usually smoked or salted. Some is exported to Kenya and Zaire, but fish is particularly important for domestic consumption, to offset protein deficiencies in the national diet.

Only about 5 percent of Uganda's population lives in urban

Picking tea on a large estate in western Uganda

areas. Kampala, the capital since independence and the largest city, has a population of just under 400,000. It is also the country's business, industrial, and cultural center and is served by the Kenya-Uganda railway and by an international jet airport located at Entebbe, twenty-one miles to the south. Entebbe, now a quiet suburb on the shore of Lake Victoria, was the British administrative center during the colonial period, while Kampala was the seat of the *kabaka* of Buganda.

Kampala and smaller urban communities house Uganda's light industries, which manufacture products such as textiles, beverages, cigarettes, and shoes for the domestic market. Cotton ginning, sugar refining, coffee, tea, and tobacco processing also are carried on. Jinja, on the northern shore of Lake Victoria

Copper smelter at Jinja on Lake Victoria

and with a population of about 100,000, is the second largest city and the site of Owen Falls Power Station, which supplies electricity to most of Uganda and to about 40 percent of Kenya. Copper, Uganda's most important mineral resource and third largest earner of foreign exchange, is smelted at Jinja. The Kilembe mines, source of the nation's copper, are located at the foot of the Ruwenzori Mountains in western Uganda, near the town of Kasese, to which a rail spur was completed in 1956. Most of Uganda's copper is exported to Japan.

The development of tourism, an important economic goal for Uganda, gained momentum with the establishment of the Uganda Tourist Board in 1968. In 1967, the luxurious Kampala International Hotel (originally named the Apolo, after the country's president at the time) was completed. With its 300 balconied rooms, outdoor swimming pool, and handsome, parklike setting, the hotel was designed to attract business and diplomatic personnel to the city, as well as visitors on the first lap of a safari through the exceptional Uganda wildlife parks in the western and northern reaches of the country. Most tours are operated by the Kampala division of the United Touring Company, an international African touring organization that works in close cooperation with the Uganda Tourist Board, Uganda National Parks, and Uganda Hotels Limited, a chain of some twenty town, resort, and wildlife-area hotels that is affiliated with the Uganda Development Corporation, a government agency. As a result of these massed efforts, tourism quadrupled between 1966, when there were 23,000 visitors, and 1972, when the number of tourists rose to nearly 100,000. The aim of the Uganda Tourist Board since its inception has been to make tourism the country's third largest earner of foreign exchange, after coffee and cotton.

Uganda's two largest national parks, Queen Elizabeth and Murchison Falls, lie in the richly scenic lake country of the Western Rift. They serve as sanctuaries not only for the mammals of the lush savannas and the green forest glades but for the reptiles, fish, and bird life of the lakes, streams, swamps, and the Nile River. Both parks are located in areas that were relatively well settled by the latter half of the nineteenth century. Then, as the result of a severe tsetse-fly infestation in the early 1900's, the human population had to be evacuated. Numbers of wild animals gradually drifted back into these regions, which at one time had been their habitat. Eventually the areas were set aside as game reserves. In 1952, both reserves were designated as national parks.

Queen Elizabeth National Park includes, among its 1500

Tree-climbing lion in Ishasha River sector
of Queen Elizabeth National Park

square miles of territory, Lake Edward and Lake George, and the twenty-four-mile Kazinga Channel that links the two. These hippo-populated waters contain a heavy concentration of fish, especially tilapia, a table fish found in many East African lakes. Today small fishing villages, with smoking and freezing facilities for the local catches of tilapia, lungfish, and catfish, exist inside the park. The inhabitants of the lakeside settlements are descendants of fishermen who lived in the region before the tsetse fly invaded it. Now, as in other wildlife areas of East

Africa, men and animals have had to make a careful compromise, living together in a shared habitat. The Ishasha River sector in the extreme southwestern corner of the park is noted for its tree-climbing lions. Groups of eight or more of the tawny beasts habitually spend the warm drowsy afternoons draped in the limbs and branches of the region's venerable wild fig trees. Queen Elizabeth National Park is rich in a variety of wildlife: topi, buffalo, Uganda kob, and elephant. The park contains a smaller variety of the world's largest land animal, also found in neighboring Zaire, that is commonly known as the Congo rat because of its runty size as compared with the East African bush elephant.

Murchison Falls National Park, which covers about 2500 square miles, encloses a large segment of the Victoria Nile and also skirts part of the Albert Nile. The shores of both portions of the great river are literally congested with animal life of immense variety, offering a glimpse of what the primeval world must have looked like. Launches that regularly cruise the Victoria Nile, on a three-hour river trip to the base of Murchison Falls, reveal the bobbing black backs of the park's multitude of hippos, which remain submerged in the shallows all day, going ashore to graze at night. Occasionally the small pointed ears, pop eyes, and massive jaw of a hippo emerge from the water, and the vast fleshy-pink mouth stretches open in what appears to be a gigantic yawn. Crocodiles, twenty feet or more long, sun themselves on the sandbanks awaiting victims. The prey usually is propelled toward the crocodile's jaws with a sweeping motion of its tail. Often the trapped creature then is dragged into the water and stowed away beneath a snug underwater ledge where no other animal can feed on it.

Uganda's newest national park, Kidepo Valley, lies in the harsh, thirsty northeastern sector of the country, in a region

Hippos in Murchison Falls National Park

inhabited by the primitive Karamojong tribesmen. It offers a
very different landscape from the moist, almost tropical settings
of the other two parks. Kidepo was given national park status
in 1962 and enlarged in 1967 to its present size of 850 square
miles. The dry sandy-bedded rivers and low rainfall of this area
led to extreme competition between wildlife and the Karamojong cattle herds, so that many wild species were being starved
or poached out of existence. Today the depleted cheetah, Bright's
gazelle, greater kudu, lesser kudu, roan antelope, zebra, eland,
dik-dik—some of which exist nowhere else in Uganda—are

coming back into their own, and expanded tourist facilities are being developed for Kidepo.

Late in 1972, as part of his policy of Africanization, President Amin changed the names of many of Uganda's parks, lakes, mountains, and city streets. Queen Elizabeth National Park was renamed Ruwenzori National Park, and Murchison Falls National Park became Kabalega National Park. Lake Edward is now Lake Idi Amin Dada, while Lake Albert is called Lake Mobutu Sesse Seko after the president of Zaire. The renaming of the two lakes, whose shores touch both Uganda and Zaire, took place in October, 1972, following a conference between the two leaders, who share similar points of view and are implementing thorough and rapid Africanization in their countries.

Favored over its East African neighbors in terms of natural resources, Uganda also has made good progress in developing its human resources. Education takes a high priority in Ugandan life today. In part, this policy is due to the work of the Christian missionaries who first appeared in Buganda in 1877 at the invitation of Kabaka Mutesa I. As learning the Bible required reading, the missionaries' teachings soon broadened to include writing, arithmetic, history, geography, and manual skills. By the turn of the century there were secondary as well as primary schools run by both Protestant and Catholic groups. Their teaching is reflected in the predominantly Christian population of Uganda today, estimated at 60 to 70 percent, with Catholics holding a majority. In fact, Uganda's large Roman Catholic population brought about a historic visit by Pope Pius VI in 1969, the first time a reigning pontiff traveled to an African country on a religious mission. Only about 6 percent of Ugandans are Moslems. Most of the remainder observe tribal religions.

There is an even earlier tradition for formal education in Uganda, for in Buganda and the other kingdoms the custom was to send selected youths to court or to the homes of the local chiefs for learning. Nowadays over 70 percent of the children between the ages of six and twelve attend Uganda's secular primary schools. Primary education, although subsidized by the government, is not free so parents must pay fees, usually $5 to $10 per year, depending on the district and whether the school is in an urban or rural area. They also must buy the required school uniform, usually a two-color outfit such as a pink blouse or shirt worn with a tan skirt or trousers. Yellow-and-blue and white-and-green are popular color combinations, too, each small school selecting its own so that its pupils are clearly identifiable. The typical East African country schoolhouse is a long single-story building with a string of classrooms, each of which is entered through its own doorway from the main courtyard or assembly ground. Often the classroom windows are without glass and permanently open to the air.

Relatively few primary-school graduates, even in education-oriented Uganda, go on to secondary school. The school fees on this level run from $50 to $150 per year, depending on the school and whether the student must board there or not. As secondary schools usually are located in urban areas, many people send their sons and daughters to live with town-dwelling relatives to save boarding fees. The town relatives often grumble but recognize this obligation as another claim of the African "extended family."

Makerere University, founded by the British as a technical school in 1921, is the oldest institution of higher learning in East Africa. In 1963, it joined with the universities in Nairobi and Dar es Salaam to become the University of East Africa. Makerere's campus occupies one of Kampala's seven green hills and has the peaceful academic atmosphere of such institutions almost anywhere in the world. It now has an enrollment of about 3000 students and offers degrees in such areas as medicine, law, philosophy, and agriculture.

English, the country's official language, is the language of instruction on all school levels with the possible exception of primary schools in remote areas where English-speaking teachers cannot be found. In that case, a tribal language such as Luganda, the principal tribal tongue and the language of the former kingdom of Buganda, may be used, but usually only up to fourth grade. Swahili, although understood by some Ugandans, never fully penetrated the country because of its inland location and so is not as commonly heard there as it is elsewhere in East Africa. The literacy rate in Uganda is judged to be between 20 and 40 percent, depending on whether the criterion is literacy in English, in Luganda, or in some other tribal language.

In the area of health, Ugandans have been victim to the usual range of East African diseases, with malaria and parasitic infections causing the greatest problem. A very prevalent nutritional disease in Uganda is kwashiorkor, caused by protein deficiency. It comes on abruptly when children are weaned from mother's milk and put on a steady diet of *matoke*, which is almost entirely carbohydrate. The symptoms—puffiness and swelling of the arms, legs, and abdomen, and a pale reddish-brown hair color due to pigmentation disturbances—may be seen in babies and toddlers in many parts of the country. With the assistance of the United Nations Children's Fund, women's groups in villages and towns have been given information on the use of protein-yielding dried beans, peanuts, and fish in the diet, in combination with *matoke* or equally starchy staples such as cassava. Those tribes that habitually eat fried termites

A health and nutrition education class for Ugandan women sponsored by
the United Nations Children's Fund and the World Health Organization

and other insects have been encouraged to include them in
meals whenever possible, as they are a good source of protein.

Kampala's Mulago Hospital, housed in expanded modern
quarters, is the largest in East Africa, with nearly 900 beds,
20,000 inpatients, and several hundred thousand outpatients a
year. By 1972, Makerere University Medical School (for which
Mulago is the teaching hospital) was graduating close to
100 doctors a year, most of whom were Asian citizens of Kenya,

Tanzania, and Uganda. Missionary-run and government-oper-
ated hospitals, health centers, and leprosariums are fairly well
distributed around the country, but clearly more facilities are
needed. The life expectancy of Ugandans, although the highest
in East Africa, is currently only forty-four years.

In the realm of foreign affairs, the regime of President Idi
Amin triggered a series of events that has made it difficult to
define Uganda's position of alignment both within the East
African Community and beyond it. The Asian-expulsion announcement of August, 1972, drew its most immediate and
overt response from neighboring Tanzania. In September, President Amin claimed that rebel Ugandan forces, under the leadership of ousted president A. Milton Obote, invaded Uganda from
Tanzania border points. President Amin retaliated with Ugandan air force bombings of Tanzanian ports on the southern
shore of Lake Victoria. Whether Obote, with a limited following
in Uganda, could reinstate himself as president, however, was
doubtful if indeed such was the intention of the attacks from
Tanzania. Relations between President Amin and President
Nyerere of Tanzania remained cool.

The official reaction from the Kenyan government to President Amin's Asian-deportation order was one of disapproval,
even though Kenya itself has a large Asian population with a
very high degree of economic dominance. While Kenya's
Deputy Minister of Home Affairs did express personal agreement with Amin's views, President Jomo Kenyatta appeared to
adhere to his traditional role as neutralist and peacemaker in
East African affairs. Kenya's chief concern was the health of the
Ugandan economy, as Kenya's exports to Uganda are considerable.

Outside Africa, Uganda's principal trading partners as of

1972 were Japan, India, Great Britain, the United States, West Germany, and Canada. Following the Asian-deportation announcement, both Great Britain and the United States decided temporarily to withhold agricultural-assistance loans and other development aid slated for Uganda. Around the world, the general state of affairs in Uganda seemed to call for suspended judgment.

The Ugandan people, like all East Africans, have been the victims of racialism through colonial domination. This past has not made them less susceptible to prejudice toward others. Indeed, because of their own experiences, they may be even more so. Uganda is not unlike other ex-colonial states all over the African continent in its striving toward Africanization. President Amin chose to use an abrupt rather than a gradual method to approach this goal. It is to be hoped that Uganda will work its way out of its twin problems of inherent tribalism and colonially bred racialism and will emerge to realize its full potential as one of Africa's most richly endowed nations.

VI
KENYA

Independent Kenya today reflects a past of rapid change and development. A no-man's land until very late in the period of African exploration, it then moved briskly toward agricultural growth at the hands of a British-planter aristocracy. It became the most thoroughly British of the East African colonial possessions, underwent a bloody independence struggle, and emerged, surprisingly, as the most moderate and carefully paced of the independent East African states. *Harambee*, the slogan of the new Kenya, is the Swahili equivalent for "all together, heave!" While the idea of "pulling together" for nationhood is aimed chiefly at Kenya's troublesome tribal rivalries, it does not exclude the idea of pulling together for a successful multiracial society as well.

Originally Great Britain had few plans for Kenya except as a means of access to Uganda and the Nile source. The building of the Kenya-Uganda railway, which was begun in 1896, a year after Britain had established its protectorate over Kenya, led to the eventual opening up of the country to Europeans. At first, even though the tribal lands appeared vast and sparsely inhabited, there was little thought of foreign settlement. Then, in 1897, Britain's Lord Delamere came to Kenya on a hunting expedition, viewed the cool green central highlands, and recommended them for European farming estates.

At that time the railroad had not even reached the site of present-day Nairobi. When it did, in 1899, the unborn town was simply a level spot in the uplands about thirty miles east of the Rift Valley escarpment. It consisted of railway-construction workshops and a crude camp for the railway laborers and supervisors. By 1901, the railroad reached Kisumu, today a Kenyan port on the eastern shore of Lake Victoria, and the British realized that they would have to develop Kenya in order to pay off the railroad's construction costs. European farmers still showed so little interest in settling in Africa that, in 1903, the British government considered using the vast open spaces of Kenya as an area of settlement for the Jews, who were without a homeland. The real productivity of the central highlands was unknown at the time.

Nevertheless, the earliest foreign settlers in Kenya were Afrikaners, white South Africans of Dutch ancestry, who arrived in 1908 and broke the virgin soil of the high plains to plant wheat. Their success encouraged British planters, who soon followed, settling over the most fertile part of the country, some seven and one-half million acres of rolling land, lying mainly to the north of the growing railway town of Nairobi. About half of this territory was suited only to cattle and sheep ranching, while the other half lent itself to mixed farming of mainly European crops and additional cash crops that throve in this part of Africa, particularly coffee.

Although the "white highlands," as this region soon came to be known, appeared empty to the settlers, it actually supported great numbers of wild animals as well as the pastoral-nomadic Masai tribesmen with their herds of cattle and the agriculturalist Kikuyu, who did not grow food much beyond subsistence requirements. The Kikuyu soon were compressed into smaller areas or "native reserves," or they gave up independent farming altogether as they went to work for the white planters on their wheat farms and coffee estates. Gradually the wildlife and the Masai with their herds left the area. The Masai turned south to the more arid lands between Nairobi and the Tanganyikan border, spilling across the border as well. Their existence in the Kenya heartland is today a rapidly fading memory, preserved in place names such as that of Kenya's capital city, Nairobi, which in the Masai language means "the place of cold water."

After World War I and the change in status from protectorate to colony in 1920, Kenya's white population swelled. British banks made agricultural loans to exservicemen and others. Although the white settlers often encountered hard work, disappointment, and loneliness, there was also cheap and plentiful African labor to do the backbreaking jobs, the land yielded up its fruits season after season, and the agricultural exports brought good prices on the world market. The 1920's, for the most part, were a time of prosperity for Kenya's white settlers. While British life was re-created in the cool Kenya highlands, complete with churches and schools, country homes and gardens, and English-style country inns, the culture of the African often was ignored entirely or was made subservient to that of the European through the introduction of Western religions and social customs. The African who had become a servant or hired hand on the European farming estate was thus separated from his tribal background.

The world depression that began in 1929 caused economic hardship among the Kenyan planters. As market prices plummeted, some closed their estates or cut their staffs drastically, sending bewildered and unskilled African laborers, their tribal affiliations broken, to Nairobi or other urban centers in search of work. The rural Africans moved into shantytown slums, their morale further shattered by the sharp social stratifications they encountered in the complex new cities, where a severe caste system separated Asians from Europeans, Africans from Asians, and even Africans from Africans.

After a time world conditions improved and the white-settler economy entered a new era of prosperity. During World War II, Kenya was an important base of operations for the British in their campaign against the Italians in Somaliland and Ethiopia. Immediately after the war, in 1946, growing Kikuyu dissatisfaction with the overpowering British regime expressed itself in the formation of the Kenya African Union, which had roots in earlier Kikuyu organizations.

As far back as 1921, with the formation of the Young Kikuyu Association, there had been agitation for the return of the Kikuyu lands taken by the white settlers. In 1925, the YKA changed its name to Kikuyu Central Association, and in 1928 Jomo Kenyatta, a young Kikuyu born near Nairobi and educated at a Church of Scotland (Presbyterian) mission school, became general secretary of the KCA. The following year he visited England as a KCA representative. Between 1932 and 1946, Kenyatta spent much time traveling, working, and studying in Europe, especially in England, where he attended the London School of Economics.

In 1947, a year after his return to Kenya, Kenyatta became

president of the Kenya African Union, which was calling for meaningful African representation on the country's Legislative Council. Although one African had been placed on the Council in 1944 (the first in British East Africa) and although two additional African representatives were added in 1946, their appointment was merely a token gesture. By the early 1950's, the KAU had enlarged and gathered sufficient strength to launch an independence movement, which alarmed the white population. Demands were made for Kenyatta's deportation.

Among the Kikuyu a secret society, utilizing the tribal ritual of taking blood oaths, erupted into a terrorist movement called the Mau Mau. Acts of violence were directed against the white settlers, the colonial administration, and against those Kikuyu who did not go along with the terrorist philosophy. On October 12, 1952, Britain declared a "state of emergency" in Kenya, and in April, 1953, Kenyatta, along with other KAU leaders, was arrested. He was charged subsequently with heading the Mau Mau movement and sentenced to prison. His jail term lasted until 1959. He then was detained in northern Kenya until 1961.

Kenyatta's sentencing unleashed a period of civil war, with numerous raids and burnings, tortures and murders, committed mainly in the Kikuyu highlands. By 1956, most of the fighting had subsided, but officially the "emergency" lasted until January 12, 1960. Although the Mau Mau terror was widely regarded as a massive bloody assault on whites living in Kenya, final statistics revealed that fewer than 100 Europeans had lost their lives during the seven-year emergency, whereas nearly 12,000 Africans had been killed, mainly Kikuyu of anti-Mau Mau sympathies.

The Mau Mau terror, brutal and wasteful of human lives, most of them African, served at least to convince the British that independence for Kenya was inevitable. Elections were scheduled, and two African parties emerged. KANU (Kenya African National Union) was Kikuyu-led but included strong Luo and Kamba representation. It favored the creation of an independent Kenya with a strong central government that would obliterate tribal differences. The opposition party, KADU (Kenya African Democratic Union) advocated *majimbo,* a system based on a federation of tribal groups, each with local autonomy. In May, 1963, KANU, which was led by Jomo Kenyatta, scored a victory in the elections, and on December 12, 1963, Kenya achieved its long-sought independence. (The name of the country was henceforth to be pronounced with a short *e,* as in Kenyatta.) A year after independence, on December 12, 1964, Kenya was declared a republic and Jomo Kenyatta became its first president.

Since independence the strong, guiding figure of President Kenyatta—lovingly and respectfully known as M'zee, Swahili for "the old one"—has been remarkably successful in welding Kenya's rival tribal peoples and diverse racial and religious groups into one nation. However, Kenya has not been without its problems of political dissent, tribalism, and racialism.

In November, 1964, KADU voluntarily dissolved and its members were absorbed into KANU, making Kenya a one-party state. But in 1966, Oginga Odinga, the vice president since independence, resigned his office and his party membership in KANU to form a left-wing opposition party, the Kenya People's Union. Odinga, a Luo elder with a strong tribal following, charged that the Kenyatta government, which was mainly Kikuyu, was too "capitalistic."

Tribalism flared when, in July, 1969, Tom Mboya, Kenya's ambitious young Economics Minister and a Luo, was gunned

Presidents Nyerere and Kenyatta, beset
with challenges but hopeful for the future

down on a busy Nairobi shopping street. His assassin was a
Kikuyu who, before he was executed, made veiled statements
implying that his orders had come from Kikuyu government
officials. Oddly enough Mboya did not have the strong support
of the Luo and was a personal enemy of the venerated Odinga.
This very division of Luo tribal loyalties was what had maintained tribal calm, since independence, between Kenya's two
million Kikuyu and one and a third million Luo, the two largest
tribal groups.

But as a martyr in death, Mboya became a tribal hero. When
President Kenyatta drove to memorial services for Mboya at

a Roman Catholic cathedral in Nairobi, his car was stoned. In October, 1969, Kenyatta ventured into the heart of Luo territory, appearing at Kisumu to dedicate a new hospital. He apparently planned the confrontation in order to test the feelings of the Luo and, if necessary, to assert his authority. When the crowd threatened the presidential limousine, Kenyatta's bodyguard fired, killing and wounding over a dozen people. Odinga, whose presence was believed to have incited the crowd, was jailed for eighteen months, and the Kenya People's Union was banned, ending the existence of any opposition party.

The months that followed were uneasy ones, as the government waited for Luo reaction. Then, in December, 1969, KANU called a parliamentary election, giving the Luo a chance to regain their influence in government. Although only one political party was permitted, any candidate could run, including members of the opposition. The election cleared the air of many grievances. Two thirds of the parliament was made up of newly elected members, including an Odinga lieutenant and several moderate younger Luo. President Kenyatta was automatically reelected by KANU to a five-year term. Kenya apparently had survived the most serious threat to its unity since becoming an independent state.

However, antigovernment plots have continued to be uncovered. In 1972, several Kenyan army and air force officers pleaded guilty to a charge of conspiracy to overthrow the government and place President Kenyatta under detention. Almost all such plots have been traced to members of the smoldering Kenya People's Union, now underground, and to Odinga himself.

President Kenyatta is now in his eighties, and the question of his successor is a matter of deep concern. According to the constitution, in the event of the president's death the vice president (now Daniel Arap Moi, a member of the Kalenjin tribe) would serve as acting president for ninety days, at which time KANU would choose a new president. It is difficult to predict whether the orderly sequence of events would take place or whether the occasion of a presidential succession would unleash vigorous tribal conflict.

In view of Kenya's strongly divided racial groups, both in the colonial era and since independence, President Kenyatta has followed a racial policy combining elements of both reform and conservatism. His approach appears to have been a practical one based on the premise that whatever is good for the economy is good for Kenya.

A first step regarding agriculture, even before independence, was the "million-acre scheme" whereby the British agreed to break up one million acres of "white highland" farmland into seven- to twenty-acre lots for the resettlement of Kikuyu and other tribal peoples of the region. The government provided loans for the Africans to purchase the farms. By the late 1960's, about 30,000 Africans were working their own farms on land that formerly had belonged to 970 Europeans. Another half million acres of white-held land was sold in holdings of twenty acres or more to prosperous Africans or to the government for development as cooperative farms.

Although the government declared in 1967 that henceforth only Kenyan citizens could "normally" own land, about four million acres of high-quality farm and ranching land (of the original seven and a half million acres taken by white settlers) still remained in European hands. The other two million acres belonged to Africans, Europeans with Kenyan citizenship, or to the Kenyan government. A more extreme leader would no doubt have had all European holdings subdivided for African

A harvest of maize, one of Kenya's basic crops

farmers, but Kenyatta recognized the value of maintaining a backbone of skilled, experienced, and productive agriculturalists in the newly independent country. The European-owned farms meant high tax revenues for the government, employment opportunities for Africans, and a continuing healthy domestic and foreign trade in agricultural products.

Coffee, which Africans were not permitted to grow during the colonial era until after the Mau Mau rebellion, is the most important export crop and Kenya's principal earner of foreign exchange. Maize, wheat, and other cereals are grown mainly for domestic consumption, although some are exported, as are meat and dairy products, largely to other African countries.

A Kikuyu family gathering pyrethrum flowers,
which are made into an insecticide

Sisal and pyrethrum are popular cash crops developed during
the colonial era. But as the fibers of the sisal plant now can be
closely duplicated by synthetics, and chemicals for insecticides
can be manufactured easily in laboratories, these crops have
been dropping in value. Coffee, which fluctuates sharply in
price on the world market, long has been a risk as a single
major export, so Kenya farmers have been diversifying in recent
years with the growing of tea, sugar, cotton, and rice, and, to
a lesser degree, pineapples and cashew nuts.

About 88 percent of Kenya's population is engaged in agriculture, although only about 12 percent of the country's 225,000
square miles of territory is well-suited for farming. Another

5½ percent is well-suited for stockraising. The northern three fifths of the country is mostly arid, thorny scrubland of extremely low productivity. Parts of northern Kenya have a population density as low as two persons per square mile. The average for the country is forty-four and runs much higher in many areas of the relatively fertile southern two fifths.

Agriculture plays only a partial role in Kenya's economy. Reversing the situation that exists in Tanzania and Uganda, Kenya derives most of its gross national product not from farming and herding but from industry. Although not an industrial nation by any means, light industry is well developed, supplying a wide range of consumer goods and other products for domestic use, such as building materials. Kenya's industries also process agricultural products, largely for export, and there is a large oil refinery at Mombasa that processes crude petroleum imported from the countries of the Persian Gulf. Kenya has no oil or mineral wealth of its own.

Business and industry have been the province of Kenya's European and Asian populations. Of Kenya's 11 million people, about 97 percent are Africans. The remaining 3 percent are Indians, Arabs, and Europeans (mainly British). While the latter two groups probably number fewer than 50,000 each, Kenya's Indian population (including Pakistanis and Goans) is estimated at about 200,000. As elsewhere in East Africa, the overwhelming number of wholesale and retail businesses have been owned by Indians, and most of the doctors, lawyers, teachers, and other professionals have been Indian. The 1960's did see a drive to Africanize in the wake of Kenyan independence or at least to Kenyanize: direct the economy into the hands of Kenyan citizens, whether African, Asian, or European in origin. This policy was implemented mainly through the restriction of business licenses to citizens only. As a result, about 20,000 Kenyan Asians with British passports emigrated to Great Britain in the late 1960's, at which time Britain cut down its admission quota to 3500 Asian families a year. At present Africanization is still an avowed policy, but the government frowns on "window dressing," a practice whereby Asian firms hire an African manager or other executive who is not qualified but merely occupies a token position. Such use of African employees is meaningless and damages the African's self-esteem. The government recognizes that Africans still are not ready to take over in a number of areas, such as the government's own Ministry of Health, which admits it is a long way from Africanization because of the shortage of trained medical personnel.

By using moderation with Asian businessmen and professionals, as he has with European farmowners, President Kenyatta is getting the best for the Kenyan economy. Indian entrepreneurs pay taxes, employ Africans in jobs they *can* fill competently, develop trade, and help, along with British commercial interests, to provide the 50 percent of gross national product that Kenya derives from its businesses and industries. This policy may not be the African dream, but for the present it has marked practical advantages. Of course, the majority of Asians and British living and working in Kenya today have taken Kenyan citizenship.

Most of Kenya's business and industrial activity is based in its major cities. Nairobi, the mile-high capital and largest city, now has a population of about half a million and is growing rapidly. It is the administrative, commercial, and cultural center of Kenya and also serves as a hub for all of East Africa. The East African Railways system, which today connects Kenya, Tanzania, Uganda, and adjacent countries with over 3600 miles of rail service, has its headquarters in Nairobi. Even more important is Nairobi's Embakasi Airport, which is served by a host of international and local airlines. Trans World Airlines flies into Nairobi from New York, 7356 air miles away, while local flights from as close as Arusha (175 miles away, across the Tanzania border) buzz in and out several times a day. A totally cosmopolitan city with its shops and safari outfitters, its restaurants and hotels, Nairobi recently has added a new seventeen-story Hilton Hotel, which dominates the skyline. The Nairobi Hilton attracts travelers on both business and pleasure trips, for the city is the starting point for most East African safaris, whether of the photographic or hunting variety.

Nairobi, hub of East Africa, receiving some of the thousands of tourists landed each week by TWA and other international airlines

Mombasa, Kenya's second largest city, with about 250,000 people, lies on the Indian Ocean 320 miles east of Nairobi and has a multiracial population typical of East African coastal cities. The streets and markets are thronged with men in *kanzus*, shorts, and business suits, frequently worn with Moslem skull-caps or Indian turbans. Women who do not wear Western garments are seen in the Indian sari, the African *kitenge*, or the Moslem *boui-boui*, a modest black coverall with a long billowing skirt and a hood or headscarf of the same shiny lightweight black fabric.

The structures that line the traffic-congested streets convey Arabic, Indian, and European-colonial influences, overlaid with the grimy defacings of heavy commerce. The old Arab quarter and the old dhow harbor still exist, but the modern harbor with its important rail connections is what makes Mombasa a vital shipping center and Kenya's chief port. Mombasa was the seat of British administration until 1907 when the construction of the railroad enabled the government to move inland to cooler and more centrally located headquarters at Nairobi.

Tourism challenges coffee in its importance to the Kenyan economy. Today 12 percent of the country's foreign exchange income stems from tourism. Not until the 1950's, however, did the British colonial authorities begin to recognize the importance of setting aside game reserves and national parks so that Kenya's wildlife, heretofore thoughtlessly sacrificed to the expansion of cattle ranches and farming estates or indiscriminately hunted for sport, could be preserved from extinction. A very important factor favoring a national park system was the prospect of commercial profit to be derived from British colonial investment in a Kenyan tourist industry. Since independence, British Kenyans have continued to operate most of Kenya's strikingly handsome safari lodges, as well as its luxurious Indian Ocean beach-resort

Mombasa, a jumble of Arabic, Indian, and
European influences on the East African coast

hotels. Although impressive African-owned hotels and lodges
are beginning to appear and the government now is training
Africans for managerial and administrative hotel posts, little
direct effort is being made to oust the highly successful non-
African hoteliers and tour operators.

Tsavo National Park, in southeastern Kenya, is today the
largest game park of its kind in the world. It covers 8000 square
miles and has a varied animal population including about
20,000 elephants. The Tsavo area became notorious in the late
1890's when the first 150 miles of railroad tracks were being
laid to the upcountry from Mombasa. A group of man-eating
lions preyed upon the construction workers for many months.
Scores of laborers were killed, and one diabolical lion actually

entered a railway carriage halted at a siding and made off with the British superintendent of railway police, who, armed with a gun, had fallen asleep while waiting for the marauding beasts to appear. For years afterward, the "man-eaters of Tsavo" continued to provide an excellent excuse for the unrestricted killing of lions by European sportsmen, not only in Kenya but in the Serengeti.

Tsavo National Park today shows the effects of East Africa's disrupted ecology due to the encroachment of man. Despite its great size, the park does not appear to be large enough for its protected and growing elephant population. By nature, elephants roam over vast land areas. Their prodigious appetite requires several hundred pounds of vegetation per day. Due to conditions of recurrent drought and overpopulation, reeds and grasses are not adequate, so elephants turn to eating the bark of acacia trees or tearing open the trunks of venerable baobab trees to get at the pithy fiber that lies underneath. Parts of Tsavo, strewn with trees dead from barkstripping, are dying landscapes that resemble battlefields.

The baobab, one of East Africa's most remarkable trees, may live 900 years or longer and is vital to a host of small animals and birds, as well as bees and other insects. The tree has a huge trunk, thirty feet in diameter at maturity, but spindly, twisted, bare-looking branches that resemble roots. For this reason Africans say that God must have been angry at the baobab tree, for he thrust it into the ground upside down.

As Tsavo is in a low-rainfall region, the elephants' destruction of trees that have no chance to regenerate eventually may transform the landscape into a semidesert. This prospect raises the question of scientifically cropping the herds, which has been undertaken from time to time by the Kenyan government. Elephant tusks are sold through the official ivory-auction ware-

A baobab tree, many hundreds of years old, with branches
that look like a root system when viewed upside down

house at Mombasa. A tusk of a mature elephant weighs about
thirty-five kilograms, or over seventy pounds, and brings $90 to
$100 a pound. Elephant tusks sell mainly to Japan, India, and
other Asian countries for carving, but a program is now under
way to teach ivory carving to Kenyans.

Two game reserves in southern Kenya, lying close to the Tanzanian border, are Amboseli and Masai Mara. Kenya's game
reserves differ from its national parks, as the authorities permit
the Masai to live and graze their cattle, sheep, and goats on the
reserve. Although the Masai do not kill wild animals unless
their cattle are attacked by them, these "combined-living" areas
show the results of crowding in East Africa.

Amboseli Game Reserve's 1250 square miles consist largely

Two seventy-pound elephant tusks awaiting
auction at the Mombasa ivory warehouses

of a dry lake bed of short grass, thorn, and scrub. The close-
cropped flats, swirling with ashen-white dust in the dry season,
are shared by zebra, wildebeest, buffalo, rhino, leopard, lion,
and the ever-increasing domestic herds of the Masai. Masai
Mara Game Reserve consists of 650 square miles, directly
adjoining Tanzania's Serengeti National Park. As the wildlife
here has free access to the Serengeti, the competition for grazing land between the Masai herds and the wild animals is not
as marked.

Nairobi National Park, lying only five miles from the heart of
downtown Nairobi, serves as a natural wildlife "zoo" both for
quick visitors to the capital and for Africans who live in the
city. This forty-four-square-mile game park contains a generous

sampling of the animals that once roamed freely where Nairobi now stands. The park is fenced only on its eastern, or Nairobi, side, giving the animals free access to open country for migration. On Sundays, the automobiles and minibuses are often bumper to bumper and even converge deep in the untracked bush for interesting sights such as a mother cheetah and her five cubs contemplating the evening's kill, with waiting jackals circling at their heels. Nairobi schoolchildren, many of whom would have no contact with their country's wildlife otherwise, are frequent visitors to the park and to its animal orphanage where baby and young animals can be lovingly studied and revisited.

In Aberdare National Park, in the Kenya highlands 100 miles north of Nairobi, stands the famous Treetops, a game-viewing lodge built forty feet above the ground in the branches of lofty

Giraffe in Nairobi National Park,
five miles distant from downtown Nairobi

fig and Cape chestnut trees, where an entire night can be spent watching elephant, rhino, buffalo, and other animals visiting the water hole and salt lick below. The original Treetops was a rustic treehouse built of wood, stones, and thatch. Princess Elizabeth slept there on the night of February 5, 1952, when her father, King George VI, died. She awoke in the morning to find herself queen of England. Treetops was burned by the Mau Mau in 1954 but was rebuilt as an enlarged and very comfortable hotel on stilts, capable of accommodating seventy guests. It since has been visited by numbers of famous people including the queen herself and an American vice president.

The mission schools that were established during the colonial period, mainly in the white-settled areas of Kenya, were largely responsible for the widespread interest in education among

The water hole at Treetops, Kenya's famed game-viewing lodge

Kenyans today. It is estimated that among the Kikuyu, who were most exposed to missionary education, nearly all children now attend primary school. For other parts of the country the figure ranges between 40 and 80 percent. Among the Luo, who live on the eastern shore of Lake Victoria, 53 percent of primary-age children attend school.

The mission schools influenced the religious preferences of Kenyans. As in Uganda, the proportion of Christians in the population is high—about 60 percent. However, in Kenya, Protestants predominate over Roman Catholics. Of the remaining population, 6 percent are Moslems, and the rest are Hindus, Sikhs, and members of tribal religions.

Although the government pays about 80 percent of the cost of public primary education, parents must pay the rest in the form of school fees. The maximum for a primary-school pupil is about $15 a year. On the secondary level, public education is so costly for the government that it has encouraged the development of *harambee* schools, institutions built by the communities with local funds and contributions. There are now about 500 *harambee* secondary schools in Kenya. The plan is for the government to take over the schools once they have been on their own for a while and to add teaching personnel and physical improvements. At present, it is able to take over only about thirty such schools each year. For every ten students who enter primary school only about one enters secondary school.

In recent years employment opportunities for students with academic-course backgrounds have been decreasing, and the stress in secondary and higher education has been on technical courses. The top government institution for this purpose is Nairobi's Kenya Polytechnic Institute, which offers technical and vocational training, including hotel management. The Institute now has about 2000 students. Kenya's highest institution of

A multiracial student group at a technical high school in Nairobi

learning, the University of Nairobi, also has 2000 students. It is part of the University of East Africa, along with Makerere University and the University of Dar es Salaam.

English and Swahili are Kenya's principal languages, but the Kikuyu and Luo tribal tongues also are spoken widely. Most educational instruction is in English. However, Swahili is a compulsory subject in primary and secondary schools. Radio broadcasts beamed by the national radio station, Voice of Kenya, reach into most primary schools where they are used as a teaching aid and for adult literacy programs as well, since seventy-five to eighty percent of Kenya's population is still illiterate. Radio and television programs are about equally divided between English and Swahili. Kenya has had television since 1962.

Kenya's health problems are reflected in the low life expectancy of its people—forty-three years—similar to that of Uganda and slightly higher than that of Tanzania. An extremely serious problem for Kenya has been its soaring birth rate. Forty-eight percent of the population is now under the age of fifteen. This situation has affected nutritional health, created a need for more health services as well as schools, is leading to high unemployment rates, and portends an even greater birth rate in the very near future.

On the whole, Kenya has enjoyed good relations with foreign countries since independence, with the temporary exception of its neighbor Somalia. In 1964, Somalia urged that the 275,000 Somali nomads occupying land in northeastern Kenya be allowed "self-determination," or the right to secede and become part of Somalia. The Kenyan government refused to cede any territory. After four years of border skirmishes, Somalia dropped its claim, and in January, 1968, the two countries resumed diplomatic relations.

Kenya occupies a position of nonalignment in world affairs and joins with other independent African states in condemning colonialism in Africa. Just as President Kenyatta has managed to strike a balance between opposing elements in his own country, he has followed the role of mediator and diplomat in the East African Community and maintains cordial relations with Tanzania and Uganda despite the recently strained relationship between the two.

VII
TODAY AND
TOMORROW

Contemporary East Africa is a complex community of three alike yet dissimilar developing nations. Each is trying to define its present and map its future, but the past is never far behind. Tribalism, colonialism, racialism, illiteracy, poverty, disease, and overpopulation loom ready to shatter whatever fragile structures the new nations have built. Education, urbanization, and Africanization seem to be important and useful goals; yet careful examination of them reveals many pitfalls. Even the hope for a cooperative and constructive sharing in the post-independence years, based on common backgrounds and common problems, has proved a mockery.

In 1961, at the time of Tanganyikan independence and in anticipation of independence for Uganda and Kenya, Great Britain set up the East African Common Services Organization.

It replaced the East African High Commission established in 1948 and broadened that organization's functions and services. In addition to transportation, telecommunications and postal services, health, agricultural and industrial development, the EACSO was to have charge of currency, customs regulations, tariffs, and taxes for the three countries.

By June, 1963, there were strong sentiments among the three East African countries for political federation as well. It was to be achieved at the end of the year when Kenya became independent. A constitution for a united Kenya, Tanganyika, and Uganda was drawn up, and the United Nations was to assist in the political restructuring.

By October, 1963, however, Uganda blocked action on the federation. The Kabaka of Buganda feared that his power in the Ugandan government (already threatened by Prime Minister Milton Obote) would diminish considerably in a larger political unit. Also, Uganda as a whole was concerned that as the smallest nation it would have the least representational strength. Tanganyika, too, was beginning to have doubts about the federation. It felt that Kenya, as the most economically developed country, braced by heavy British investment, would tend to dominate the others. As a result, further preparations for political federation came to a halt, and the union never was realized.

Even economic cooperation between the three soon appeared to be one-sided and unworkable. Under the EACSO, trade among Kenya, Tanganyika, and Uganda was conducted on a tariff-free basis, while all incoming external goods were subject to a tariff. This common-market idea, by means of which goods passed among the three countries without duty payments, seemed fine in theory. But in practice a number of problems developed. Kenya, the most industrially advanced nation, was selling goods to Tanganyika and Uganda at higher prices than they would have had to pay for imports from countries outside East Africa. Yet, under the terms of the agreement, they were forced to buy these products from within the EACSO countries. In addition, the two poorer countries were losing the revenue from customs duties that they would have been collecting on foreign-bought goods.

Clearly changes were required, and in April, 1963, representatives of the three countries met to draw up the Kampala Agreement. It provided that new industries for the East African market should be developed in Tanganyika and Uganda and that companies with branches in all three countries should discontinue their operations in Kenya, thus shifting employment opportunities and commercial advantages to the other two. The agreement also permitted an EACSO country with a large trade deficit to restrict the intake of goods from another EACSO country.

Although the Kampala Agreement was never ratified, it laid the groundwork for the East African Community, which was established by treaty on June 7, 1967, by Presidents Kenyatta, Nyerere, and Obote. On December 1, 1967, the EAC went into operation. For one thing, it decentralized the old EACSO, which had been headquartered in Nairobi. Only East African rail and air transport were left in that city. Postal and telecommunications operations and the central development bank were relocated in Kampala, while control of harbors and shipping was transferred to Dar es Salaam. The EAC administrative headquarters were established at Arusha, in northern Tanzania.

A new trade agreement was drawn up. An EAC country with a large trade deficit could not restrict goods from another, but it could impose a transfer tax. Technically this tax was not the same as a tariff, such as that imposed on non-EAC countries, but it did serve to keep a fairer trade balance and to some degree, helped Tanzania and Uganda develop some industries that sold to their own domestic market.

Today the old EACSO functions, such as the issuing of currency and postage stamps and the fixing of tariff regulations on foreign goods, have been taken over by the individual countries. Now the EAC seems to be experiencing further pressures for decentralization of control. With each country working toward its own brand of economic development—Tanzania toward agrarian socialism; Uganda toward revolutionary Africanization of its business sector; Kenya toward a very gradual Kenyanization of its flourishing economy with strong colonial roots—it seems doubtful that the East African Community can be expected to play a really strong role economically in the East Africa of the foreseeable future.

In addition to its political and economic concerns, East Africa has a number of social concerns for today and tomorrow.

One is how to train the youth of the three nations. In East Africa, the image of the educated African in the white-collar job dies hard. Educators and other leaders shake their heads wearily at this ideal, which was held up before African eyes by the colonialists for three quarters of a century. Today, they complain, everybody wants to be a government minister, but there are not enough jobs for the university graduate with an academic background and a degree in political science.

Moreover, the political-science students have been held responsible lately for the relatively mild student riots that have occurred at East African universities. In 1972, when fifty-five Nairobi University students were brought up on charges for having erected barricades on a main thoroughfare (where they had been agitating for the installation of traffic lights), a mem-

Traditionalist Kikuyu women with shaved heads
and stretched earlobes attending a literacy class

ber of Parliament remarked that university education appeared
to be a waste of money, as the students were becoming "hooli-
gans." Another speaker, however, stated that money spent on
engineering and science students was worthwhile; only political-science students found time to strike.

Even young people without a university education tend to
seek nonexistent jobs. With a few years of primary schooling
and perhaps some secondary-school background, they leave the
farm areas where they were born and head for the towns, hop-

ing to obtain clerical or service jobs. Urban drift brings numbers of semieducated Africans to cities like Nairobi, where the naive and discouraged often fall in with bad companions. Purse snatching, auto thefts, and other crimes have been mounting steadily in East Africa's urban centers.

In Tanzania, President Nyerere has indicated clearly that the first order of business for youth is to remain on the land and develop *ujamaa* villages. In Kenya and Uganda, the stress on getting a secondary-school education points to urban goals, particularly when parents do not require additional field help on their small farms and when the "extended family" expects achievement, with suitable financial reward, from at least some of its members. Young Africans, caught in the conflict between families that say "go" and urban authorities that say "stay away—there are no jobs here," are an uneasy lot.

Children of polygynous marriages have trouble getting any education at all. As primary schooling is not free in the East African countries, the father who has numerous offspring is hard pressed to pay the required fees. As a result, the children do not attend school. Occasionally one hears of a prosperous African, with half a dozen wives and a great many children, who builds a schoolhouse and hires several teachers to instruct his own family. However, such cases are rare. More often, the well-to-do African gives up polygyny and restricts the number of children for which he is financially responsible. He recognizes that even with a fairly good income he can provide quality educations for only a very few offspring. Some observers feel that polygyny is decreasing and will continue to do so as more and more people start to send their children to school and come up against the problem of how to find the money to pay fees for a large brood.

Polygyny is but one expression of the position of women in

East Africa. A number of factors have conspired to make their status a lowly one. Because the infant-mortality rate is higher for males, there are more women in society, and polygyny has been a means of female survival in a primitive environment. Most tribal institutions favor males—in marriage, divorce, inheritance, property rights, and other legal matters. Colonialism put pressures on the African male, which increased the exploitation of the African female. Job competition from Asians and Europeans narrowed economic opportunity for the African wage-earner and usually meant a life of poverty and hardship for his wife.

For the average African man, independence did not work the hoped-for miracle. Most did not experience overnight economic betterment. No longer able to blame the political setup, some became demoralized, transferring economic responsibility to the already overburdened African woman. As to those Africans who have risen economically or politically since independence, most are men, and they are not anxious to share their newfound power and authority with women.

It is difficult for an East African woman to earn the necessary qualifications for economic independence, to say nothing of political leadership. While many primary schools today have an enrollment of girls equal to that of boys, the proportion changes drastically on the secondary-school and university levels. In Kenya, for example, less than one third of the secondary-school pupils and less than one quarter of the university students are females. However, these figures still indicate some progress.

When women are educated for careers, they usually are directed into nursing, domestic science, and other fields based on traditional female roles. The idea of women doctors, lawyers, and engineers is unacceptable to most East African men. When East African women do work, in either the public or private

A Ugandan woman doctor, a rarity in East Africa

sectors of the economy, they receive less pay than men do for the same or similar job, and provision is seldom made for the care of children of working mothers. Certainly progress toward the goal of Africanization would be much more rapid if both sexes could be mobilized.

In sexual and marital matters, the East African woman submits to customs and standards fixed by a male-dominated society. Although men have greater employment opportunities, they are not legally responsible nor are they considered to be morally responsible for children born out of wedlock. Thus, the woman is almost invariably the victim of any sexual indiscretion. Traditionalism often operates, too, against the educated woman who marries. Frequently an otherwise enlightened husband will require a university-trained wife to remain at home in the wife-and-mother role after marriage.

Today the influence of Westernization (much of it the result of colonialism) penetrates deeply into East African culture, most observably in the cities and towns. Often Western culture combines with African institutions to produce a jarring, uncomfortable note. East Africans are in a state of social transition, but their destination is not generally clear.

They are increasingly given to self-criticism. Letters and articles appearing in newspapers, such as Kenya's lively and popular *Daily Nation*, call for African women to stop aping their Western sisters in the use of skin-lightening creams and in the wearing of Afro or Western Caucasian wigs. On the other hand, government leaders have launched campaigns to put their more primitive tribesmen into shirts, trousers, and shoes. President Amin of Uganda has urged the Karamojong to clothe their nakedness "in the interests of the republic," while President Nyerere of Tanzania has replaced the picture of a half-naked Masai warrior that appeared on the country's hundred-shilling note with that of a cornfield. Local authorities have threatened insufficiently clad Masai with jail sentences.

In July, 1972, Kenya's attorney general, an enlightened Kikuyu (himself about to marry a young British woman, the Kenya-born daughter of Christian missionaries), defended the wearing of miniskirts as the right of the African woman to

choose to dress as she pleased. At the same time, in President
Amin's Uganda seven women (including the wife of the former
Ugandan ambassador to France and two schoolteachers) were
fined for wearing miniskirts that measured from four to six
inches above the knee, and the virtues of the suitably modest
busuti, Uganda's "national dress," were officially recommended.

Many of East Africa's young intellectuals urge a rediscovery
of traditional song, dance, and legend. Yet urban Africans
flock to Western "discos" and drive-in movies—and many rural
Africans long to be able to do the same.

Food tastes also have been affected by foreign influences.
Soon after the turn of the century, the old-fashioned African
maize vendor selling hot, charcoal-roasted ears of corn to pas-
sersby in the towns began to receive competition from the
samosa vendor. This street snack, introduced by the Indians, is
a pastry turnover filled with hotly seasoned meat and vegetables.
Prosperous Africans ate British bacon and eggs for breakfast
and steamed pudding with custard sauce for dessert. Tea became almost a national institution in the East African countries,
and the smallest villages soon had their beer-drinking establish-
ments with names like Happy Bar and Good Luck Bar related,
although distantly, to the British pub. Today the international
fast-food industry is invading East Africa. In 1972, Kentucky
Fried Chicken and the Wimpy hamburger chain added branches
in Nairobi.

For the average African, the "gifts" of colonialism have been
small indeed. Even Kenya's relative prosperity is only a thin
veneer, directly beneficial to a small segment of the population
—a mainly non-African segment at that. The statistics for poverty, illiteracy, disease, infant mortality, and adult life expectancy tell the real story for the overwhelming mass of East Africans and show them to be almost as poorly off as the people of

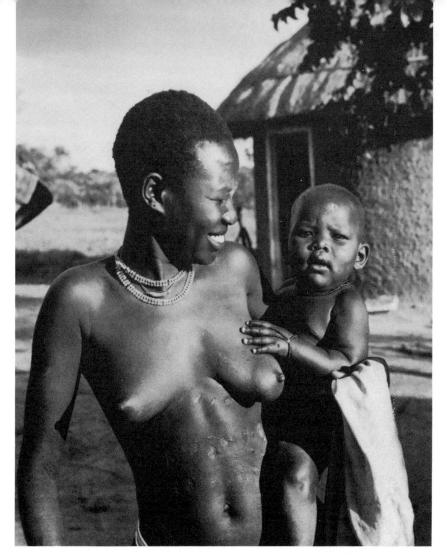

A child afflicted with the puffy body and pale reddish hair brought
on by protein-deficiency disease, still rampant in East Africa

neighboring Ethiopia, an African nation with a largely un-
tapped agricultural potential that never has been colonized at
all.

Although sharply observant East Africans apply healthy cri-
ticism to their countrymen's pursuit of Western ideals, East
Africa cannot go back to its tribal past. It must go forward. But

An East African youth, symbol of the future,
scanning a newspaper in a university reading room

cultural confusion and personal bewilderment appear to be included in the price it must pay for a colonization and an ensu-
ing Westernization it never asked for.

On the positive side, East Africa today has its treasured
political independence. Each country is a sovereign state. Each
is a member of the United Nations and of the Organization of
African Unity, which was formed in 1963 and is dedicated to

solidarity among its member states and to the elimination of colonialism in Africa.

Politically the three East African countries have not modeled themselves after the Western democracies. Kenya, Tanzania, and Uganda are one-party states, and none has had a popular election for president since independence. But the East African countries have their own special circumstances, very different from those of the West.

Today's East African leaders still are groping toward stability and a workable form and system of government. Their task is difficult, made more so because their people seem to be calling for government policies that tend to cancel each other out. They want a government strong enough to maintain national sovereignty but decentralized enough to permit autonomy for special groups. They want free universal education but low taxes. They want a flourishing Western type of economy but no foreign economic intrusion. The leader must juggle to give priority to those goals deemed most important while placating opposition groups in government and keeping the confidence of a populace often swayed by hearsay and tribal pressure.

Nationhood was just one more Western idea imposed on East African peoples by the colonial powers. But, finally, this idea yielded up independence. The task for Kenya, Tanzania, and Uganda, in the years since independence, has been for each to define its own African dream. The task for tomorrow is to realize that dream.

BIBLIOGRAPHY

Adamson, Joy, *The Peoples of Kenya*. New York: Harcourt, Brace & World, Inc., 1967

Bolton, Kenneth, *Harambee Country: A Guide to Kenya*. London: Geoffrey Bles, 1970

Dinesen, Isak, *Out of Africa*. New York: The Modern Library, Inc., 1952

Grzimek, Bernhard and Michael, *Serengeti Shall Not Die*. New York: E. P. Dutton & Co., Inc., 1961

Herrick, Allison Butler, and others, *Area Handbook for Tanzania*. Washington: U.S. Government Printing Office, 1968

Herrick, Allison Butler, and others, *Area Handbook for Uganda*. Washington: U.S. Government Printing Office, 1969

Huxley, Elspeth, *With Forks and Hope*. New York: William Morrow and Company, Inc., 1964

Matthiessen, Peter, and Eliot Porter, *The Tree Where Man Was Born: The African Experience*. New York: E. P. Dutton & Co., Inc., 1972

Moorehead, Alan, *No Room in the Ark*. New York: Harper and Row, Publishers, 1959

Moorehead, Alan, *The White Nile*. New York: Harper and Row, Publishers, 1960

Speke, John Hanning, *Journal of the Discovery of the Source of the Nile*. London: Everyman's Library, Dent, 1969

Turnbull, Colin M., *Tradition and Change in African Tribal Life*. Cleveland and New York: World, 1966

van Pelt, P., *Bantu Customs in Mainland Tanzania*. Tabora (Tanzania): T.M.P. Book Department, 1971

INDEX

Lila Perl was born and educated in New York City, and she holds a B.A. degree from Brooklyn College. In addition, she has taken graduate work at Teachers College, Columbia University, and at the School of Education, New York University. She is the author of four books for adults and nine books for children, both fiction and nonfiction. Several of them concern life in other lands. In preparation for writing *East Africa*, Miss Perl traveled extensively in Kenya, Tanzania, and Uganda, doing research at first-hand and taking many photographs. Her husband, Charles Yerkow, is also a writer, and they live in Beechhurst, N. Y.